SHAKESPEARE IN BRIEF

Concise Summaries of Plots, Characters, and Themes from All Shakespearean Plays in One Comprehensive Book

Caleb J. Sullivan

CONTENTS

INTRODUCTION:

"Shakespeare in Brief" invites you to quickly and simply explore Shakespeare's world. We've reduced the plays while retaining their richness, so you can easily grasp their core. Join us as we delve into Shakespeare's ageless works.

- Caleb J. Sullivan

DATING OF PLAYS

The chronological order of Shakespeare's plays remains a topic of scholarly debate. The current consensus is built upon a combination of various data points, including publication information (such as dates from title pages), known performance dates, as well as insights from contemporary diaries and other records. While each play can be attributed a narrow range of dates, it's impossible to definitively pinpoint the year any of Shakespeare's plays were written. Even when precise performance dates are known, little can be confidently stated about when each play was composed.

Further complicating matters is the fact that many of Shakespeare's plays exist in multiple editions, making it even more challenging to determine when official versions were finalized. For instance, multiple versions of "Hamlet" survive, three of which were printed in the First Quarto, Second Quarto, and First Folio. The version printed in the Second Quarto is the longest "Hamlet" rendition, though it omits over 50 lines found in the First Folio version. Modern scholarly editions of the play incorporate material from multiple sources.

Establishing the precise order of composition and performance of Shakespeare's plays is a challenge, and as a result, it's a subject of frequent debate. The dates listed below are approximate and based on a general consensus regarding when the plays were first staged:

1. "Henry VI, Part 1" (1589–1590)

2. "Henry VI, Part 2" (1590–1591)

3. "Henry VI, Part 3" (1590–1591)

4. "Richard III" (1592–1593)

5. "The Comedy of Errors" (1592–1593)

6. "Titus Andronicus" (1593–1594)

7. "The Taming of the Shrew" (1593–1594)

8. "Two Gentlemen of Verona" (1594–1595)

9. "Love's Labour's Lost" (1594–1595)

10. "Romeo and Juliet" (1594–1595)

11. "Richard II" (1595–1596)

12. "A Midsummer Night's Dream" (1595–1596)

13. "King John" (1596–1597)

14. "The Merchant of Venice" (1596–1597)

15. "Henry IV, Part 1" (1597–1598)

16. "Henry IV, Part 2" (1597–1598)

17. "Much Ado About Nothing" (1598–1599)

18. "Henry V" (1598–1599)

19. "Julius Caesar" (1599–1600)

20. "As You Like It" (1599–1600)

21. "Twelfth Night" (1599–1600)

22. "Hamlet" (1600–1601)

23. "The Merry Wives of Windsor" (1600–1601)

24. "Troilus and Cressida" (1601–1602)

25. "All's Well That Ends Well" (1602–1603)

26. "Measure for Measure" (1604–1605)

27. "Othello" (1604–1605)

28. "King Lear" (1605–1606)

29. "Macbeth" (1605–1606)

30. "Antony and Cleopatra" (1606–1607)

31. "Coriolanus" (1607–1608)

32. "Timon of Athens" (1607–1608)

33. "Pericles" (1608–1609)

34. "Cymbeline" (1609–1610)

35. "The Winter's Tale" (1610–1611)

36. "The Tempest" (1611–1612)

37. "Henry VIII" (1612–1613)

38. "Two Noble Kinsmen" (1612–1613)

AUTHORSHIP CONTROVERSIES

Another contentious aspect of Shakespeare's bibliography revolves around whether the Bard was indeed the sole author of all the plays associated with his name. In the 19th century, certain literary historians popularized the so-called "anti-Stratfordian theory," suggesting that Shakespeare's plays were actually the works of Francis Bacon, Christopher Marlowe, or perhaps a group of playwrights. However, subsequent scholars have debunked this theory and now widely agree that Shakespeare, the man born in Stratford-upon-Avon in 1564, did, in fact, pen all the plays attributed to him.

Nonetheless, compelling evidence exists that some of Shakespeare's plays were collaborative efforts. In 2016, a group of scholars analyzed all three parts of "Henry VI" and concluded that there was indeed the hand of Christopher Marlowe in the work. In future editions of the play published by Oxford University Press, Marlowe will be credited as a co-author.

Another play, "The Two Noble Kinsmen," was co-written

with John Fletcher, who also collaborated with Shakespeare on the lost play "Cardenio." Some scholars speculate that Shakespeare might have also collaborated with George Peele, an English playwright and poet; George Wilkins, an English playwright and innkeeper; and Thomas Middleton, a prolific writer of various dramatic works, including comedies, tragedies, and masques.

HENRY VI, PART 1 (1589–1590)

Act 1: War of the Roses

Scene 1: The Clash of Claims

Duke of Somerset and Richard Plantagenet (Duke of York) engage in a heated argument over their claims to the throne's inheritance. Somerset asserts Henry VI's right to the throne, while York contends his own legitimate claim.

Scene 2: Diplomacy and Bravery

Henry VI, along with the French King Charles and others, discusses the possibility of a long-term truce between England and France. Talbot, Engler, and others recount their military triumphs and achievements.

Scene 3: Defiance in Orleans

Talbot leads a valiant battle against the French in Orleans. Despite the French's fierce attack, Talbot stands his ground, defending the town and its inhabitants.

Scene 4: Victorious Return

After securing victory, Engler, Talbot's messenger, returns the crown to Henry VI. The king returns to London, while the ongoing power struggle between Somerset and York continues.

Scene 5: York's Aspirations

York confides his ambitions to his supporters. They decide to journey to London to present their claims before the king.

Scene 6: Royal Summit

In London, Henry VI convenes York and Somerset to address their dispute. Somerset accuses York, intensifying the conflict between them.

Scene 7: A Question of Loyalty

Suspicion arises that Henry VI might appoint Somerset as the realm's protector. Disagreeing vehemently, York leaves, and Talbot arrives to recount his military endeavors.

Scene 8: Fractured Unity

Henry VI observes the mounting discord within the kingdom and the warring factions. York, Engler, and Talbot again clash, while Henry strives to restore order.

The first act of "War of the Roses" sets the stage for the pivotal conflicts and ambitions that will shape the narrative, plunging characters into a web of power struggles and uncertainties.

Act 2: Discord and Rebellion

Scene 1: The Sorcerous Temptation

The English nobility finds itself torn asunder, with the Duke of Gloucester, the Protector of England, embroiled in a dispute with the Duke of Winchester. To fuel his ambitions, Gloucester's wife, Eleanor, suggests employing dark magic.

Scene 2: Commoners' Revolt

Led by the charismatic Jack Cade, a group of commoners rises in rebellion against the nobility. Cade adopts the alias "John Mortimer" and promises sweeping change.

Scene 3: Rivalry and Alliances

The rivalry between York and Somerset escalates, each seeking influence over the king's decisions. Suffolk orchestrates a strategic union between Margaret of Anjou and Henry VI, solidifying connections with France.

Scene 4: A Rebellion's Surge

Cade's uprising gains momentum, and he captures the unpopular Lord Say. Holding a symbolic trial, Cade pronounces judgment and executes Say, deepening the divisions.

Scene 5: Ties and Tensions

Margaret arrives in England, capturing Henry VI's heart. Suffolk and Margaret's clandestine relationship comes to light, sowing seeds of resentment among the nobles.

Scene 6: Ambitions in Motion

York assembles a following to counter Somerset's influence. Simultaneously, Cade's rebellion gains ground as he captures London, emerging as a significant threat to the crown.

Scene 7: Unmasking Rebellion

The true widow of Mortimer confronts Cade, who initially posed as her husband. Cade sheds his disguise, asserting his true identity and his rebellion against the established order.

Scene 8: Clashing Factions

York's adherents clash with Somerset's supporters, heightening tensions and setting the stage for forthcoming political and military confrontations.

Scene 9: Quelling the Storm

Henry VI returns to England, suppressing Cade's rebellion. This act accentuates the intensifying chaos and divisions within the realm, as political intrigue and social upheaval escalate.

Act 3: Wars and Alliances

Scene 1: Throne of Contention

The Duke of York directly challenges King Henry VI, asserting his rightful claim to the throne. Margaret intervenes passionately, advocating for her husband's legitimacy, igniting fiery debates.

Scene 2: Clash of Rivals

The intensifying conflict between York and Lancaster prompts both sides to gather forces for an impending battle. Their armies converge at St. Albans, culminating in the First Battle of St. Albans.

Scene 3: Aftermath of Battle

York emerges victorious and captures King Henry VI. He confronts the king over his misrule. Queen Margaret, however, rallies her loyalists, vowing vengeance for the Lancastrian cause.

Scene 4: Debating Destiny

Nobles debate the fate of the captive king. Richard, Duke of Gloucester, supports York's claim, further stoking the flames of discord within the realm.

Scene 5: News of Conflict

Word of York's triumph and Henry's capture reverberates throughout London. Queen Margaret grieves her allies' loss and solemnly swears to exact retribution.

Scene 6: Sons of Revenge

York's sons, Edward and Richard, resolve to avenge their father's death. The turmoil escalates, foreshadowing further battles and intricate political maneuvering.

Scene 7: Renewed Struggles

Henry VI regains freedom and reunites with Margaret. The Lancastrians regroup, and the power struggle rages on, characterized by shifting allegiances.

Scene 8: Forge of Alliances

The Earl of Warwick, a pivotal Yorkist supporter, negotiates a strategic union between York and Edward IV, the Duke of York's son. This alliance reshapes the dynamics of power.

Scene 9: Perseverance Amid Turmoil

Yorkists clash anew with Lancastrians, and Warwick finds himself captured. Undeterred by setbacks, York's faction remains resolute in pursuing their claims to the throne.

Scene 10: Unfolding Drama

As the war persists, the play continues to unravel the intricate web of political aspirations, shifting alliances, and treacherous betrayals that shape the destiny of England and its royal lineage.

Act 4: Rebellion and Battle

Scene 1: The King's Palace

In the fourth act of "Henry IV, Part 1," King Henry IV and his son Prince Henry, known as Harry Hotspur, face an escalating rebellion against the crown. Harry Hotspur, leading the rebels, prepares for battle.

Scene 2: The Warning of Archibald

City rebel Archibald suspects that Harry Hotspur is planning treachery and decides to alert the king. However, King Henry IV is more concerned about the uprising led by Harry Hotspur, and Archibald is killed.

Scene 3: Preparations for Battle

King Henry IV assembles an army to confront the rebels. He orders Prince Hal to intercept Harry Hotspur, who is headed to meet him. Meanwhile, Harry Hotspur and his allies also prepare for the impending battle.

Scene 4: The Battle of Shrewsbury

The fourth act culminates in the Battle of Shrewsbury between King Henry IV's forces and the rebels led by Harry Hotspur. Harry Hotspur fights valiantly but ultimately meets his end. This battle holds pivotal importance for the further development of the conflict.

Scene 5: Royal Celebration

After the battle, King Henry IV and Prince Hal celebrate their victory. Prince Hal returns to his father with the body of the fallen Harry Hotspur. While the king rejoices in the triumph, he also feels a sense of unease about his recent rise to power and the future of the kingdom.

HENRY VI, PART 2 (1590–1591)

Act 1: Seeds of Discord

Scene 1:

The act opens with the wedding celebration of King Henry VI and Margaret of Anjou. This marriage aims to strengthen the alliance between England and France, but it becomes a source of tension and conflict as the Duke of Gloucester, a powerful noble, opposes the marriage. He is suspicious of Margaret's family and ambitions.

Scene 2:

Amidst the festivities, political intrigue is already at play. Gloucester's wife, Eleanor, manipulates the situation to gain power and influence for her family. The Cardinal Beaufort, a high-ranking church official, is concerned about Gloucester's opposition and tries to defuse the tensions.

Scene 3:

The act takes a darker turn as Gloucester is arrested on charges of treason. He is later found dead in his cell, and the circumstances of his death raise suspicions. The struggle between different noble factions, particularly the Lancastrians and Yorkists, becomes more evident. Gloucester's death adds fuel to the fire of these rivalries.

Scene 4:

The act ends with the introduction of the Duke of York, who asserts his own claim to the throne. He suggests that Henry's rule is weak and that he should be the rightful king. This sets the stage for the political conflicts and power struggles that will intensify throughout the play.

Act 2: Rising Tensions

Scene 1:

The act delves into the aftermath of Gloucester's death and the rising tensions within the court. Suffolk, who was involved in arranging the marriage between Henry VI and Margaret, faces scrutiny and criticism for his role. Suffolk's relationship with Margaret becomes a focal point of intrigue and suspicion among the nobles.

Scene 2:

Meanwhile, the rebellion led by Jack Cade gains momentum. The commoners rise against the nobility, demanding social reforms and an end to corruption. Cade's rebellion underscores the discontent among the lower classes and highlights the growing divide between different segments of society.

Scene 3:

The Duke of York openly asserts his claim to the throne and rallies supporters, further heightening the political turmoil. As these power struggles intensify, the rivalry between the Yorkists and the Lancastrians becomes more pronounced. The act portrays a fractured society where different factions are vying for control, and the tensions between them are reaching a breaking point.

Scene 4:

Suffolk's political downfall begins in this act as he is accused of treason. He is banished and eventually killed, which only exacerbates the tensions. Margaret mourns Suffolk's departure but is also determined to secure her influence in the court.

Scene 5:

Amidst all this turmoil, the act also features the comedic subplot of the fraudulent marriage between the impostor Simpcox and his wife. This subplot provides a moment of comic relief amidst the larger political drama.

Act 3: Unrest Has Erupted

Scene 1:
The act continues to explore the political unrest and power struggles in the realm. The rebellion led by Jack Cade continues to gain strength, and the commoners' grievances are highlighted as they demand justice and reform.

Scene 2:

Queen Margaret and her allies, including Clifford, work to maintain their influence over King Henry VI. The nobles are divided, with factions forming around the Queen and the Duke of York. Margaret's determination to secure her position is evident as she seeks to suppress the Yorkist faction's growing power.

Scene 3:

As the rebellion intensifies, Cade's forces threaten the stability of the monarchy. The commoners' discontent is met with violence, and the situation becomes increasingly chaotic. The Duke of York and his supporters see an opportunity to challenge the King's authority, adding to the tumultuous political climate.

Scene 4:

Amidst the rebellion, personal rivalries also come to the fore. The feud between the families of Mortimer and Clifford is explored, contributing to the overall atmosphere of conflict.

Scene 5:

The act culminates in a pivotal battle between the Yorkists and the Lancastrians at St. Albans. The Duke of York's forces clash with the King's supporters, leading to a violent confrontation. The battle results in significant casualties on both sides, and the Yorkists emerge victorious.

Act 4: Shifting Fortunes

Scene 1:

The act opens with the aftermath of the battle at St. Albans. King Henry VI is captured by the Yorkists, and the power dynamic between the factions shifts once again. The Queen and her allies work to regain control over Henry and reassert Lancastrian authority.

Scene 2:

The Duke of York, now in a position of power, attempts to consolidate his rule. However, internal conflicts among the Yorkists themselves begin to surface. Richard Plantagenet, the Duke of York, and Richard Neville, Earl of Warwick, have differing opinions on how to proceed, hinting at the instability within the Yorkist camp.

Scene 3:

Meanwhile, the Lancastrian forces regroup under the leadership of Queen Margaret and Clifford. The power struggle between the two factions continues, with battles and political maneuvering intensifying.

Scene 4:

The act also features the return of Somerset, who was previously presumed dead. His reappearance adds to the complex web of allegiances and rivalries. The struggle for control over Henry VI becomes a focal point, with both sides vying to influence his decisions.

Scene 5:

As the act progresses, the Lancastrians manage to gain the upper hand and recapture King Henry from the Yorkists. The Duke of York and his allies face defeat, and the political tide shifts once again in favor of the Lancastrians.

Act 5: Concluding Moments

Scene 1:

The act begins with internal divisions among the Lancastrians becoming more pronounced. The power struggle between Queen Margaret and her allies, notably Clifford, and the more moderate faction led by the Duke of Somerset intensifies.

Scene 2:

The commoners' unrest continues, and a group of rebels led by John Cade seeks to challenge the established order. Cade's rebellion reflects the ongoing dissatisfaction of the lower classes with the ruling elite.

Scene 3:

The Duke of York, who had previously been defeated, once again asserts his claim to the throne. His forces face off against the Lancastrians, leading to the Battle of St. Albans. In this climactic battle, Somerset is killed, and the Yorkists emerge victorious, solidifying their control over the King.

Scene 4:

The final act also features the rift between the Duke of Somerset and Clifford, culminating in a deadly confrontation. The personal animosities add to the overall tension and illustrate the emotional toll of the political conflicts.

Scene 5:

The act also highlights the broader implications of the power struggles. The social order is disrupted, and rumors spread among the commoners about the King's health and the transformation of Prince Hal (now King Henry VI).

Scene 6:

Amidst these events, Falstaff, Bardolph, and Pistol are preparing to join the King's forces. Their humorous banter and interactions provide a brief respite from the heavier political drama

HENRY VI, PART 3 (1590–1591)

Act 1: The Chaos of War

Scene 1:

The Battle of Hexham rages as Lancastrian forces led by Queen Margaret clash with Yorkist troops. The Lancastrians are defeated, and Somerset is captured. The Yorkists rejoice in their victory and discuss the fate of their captives.

Scene 2:

King Henry VI is presented as a captive before Edward, Duke of York. Margaret, grieving over her fallen allies, confronts York and Henry. Margaret's impassioned speeches reflect the turmoil and heartache of the conflict.

Scene 3:

The Lancastrians, led by Margaret and Somerset, are in disarray after their defeat. Margaret attempts to rally her remaining forces with fiery speeches, vowing to continue the fight against the Yorkists.

Scene 4:

Amidst the celebration of the Yorkist victory, Richard of Gloucester takes the opportunity to subtly showcase his ambition. He reveals his intentions through his actions and interactions, setting the stage for his future rise to power.

Act 2: The Struggle for Power

Scene 1:

Warwick and Clarence secretly plot against King Edward IV. Clarence reveals his dissatisfaction with Edward's rule, and the two discuss their plan to restore Henry VI to the throne.

Scene 2:

King Henry VI is recaptured and held in captivity. Margaret's grief and sorrow intensify as she laments the fate of her husband and her fallen allies.

Scene 3:

Edward IV's triumph over Warwick's forces is portrayed, resulting in Warwick's death on the battlefield. This scene marks a turning point in the power dynamics and the decline of the Lancastrian cause.

Scene 4:

King Henry VI is once again taken captive. The shifting fortunes of the Lancastrians and Yorkists are evident as both sides continue to grapple for control of the kingdom.

Act 3: The Rise of Richard

Scene 1:

Richard of Gloucester meticulously orchestrates events to further his own ambitions. Through manipulation and cunning, he strategically places himself in positions of influence, highlighting his capacity for manipulation.

Scene 2:

 Richard proposes to Anne, the widow of Prince Edward, whom he himself killed. This shocking proposal showcases his audacity and willingness to seize opportunities, even in the midst of tragedy.

Scene 3:

Richard eliminates potential threats to his ascendancy by orchestrating the execution of Rivers, Grey, and Vaughan. His cold-blooded determination to secure his position becomes evident in this scene.

Scene 4:

Margaret's resolve is unbroken as she raises an army and invades England once again. Her persistence and determination to fight for the Lancastrian cause are palpable.

Scene 5:

The Battle of Tewkesbury unfolds, with the Yorkists emerging victorious. The death of Prince Edward and the capture of Margaret mark a significant blow to the Lancastrians and a turning point in the conflict.

Act 4: The Downfall

Scene 1:

King Henry VI meets a tragic end as he is murdered in the Tower of London. The scene underscores the ruthlessness and brutality that have come to define the struggle for power.

Scene 2:

Richard's quest for dominance continues as he manipulates his way into becoming the Lord Protector. His cunning and manipulation are on full display as he consolidates his control.

Scene 3:

The nobles, including Buckingham and Stanley, begin to question Richard's motives and his growing influence. Suspicion and mistrust grow as Richard's intentions become clearer.

Scene 4:

Lord Hastings, a former ally of Richard, is executed on Richard's orders. This act of brutality solidifies Richard's reputation for ruthlessness and fearlessness in his pursuit of power.

Act 5: The Final Battle

Scene 1:

Richard's tyrannical rule triggers opposition, and Richmond gathers support to challenge his authority. This scene sets the stage for the ultimate confrontation between the two sides.

Scene 2:

Richard is tormented by ghosts and visions in a dream, symbolizing the guilt and remorse he feels for his past actions. This scene delves into Richard's psyche, revealing his inner turmoil.

Scene 3:

The forces of Richmond and Richard converge on the battlefield of Bosworth. The epic Battle of Bosworth Field unfolds, leading to the climactic confrontation that will determine the fate of the kingdom.

Scene 4:

The Battle of Bosworth Field reaches its dramatic conclusion. Richard is slain, and Richmond emerges victorious. With Richard's death, the era of conflict and struggle for power comes to an end.

Scene 5:

The play closes with Henry VII, Richmond, expressing hope for a new era of peace and stability as he ascends to the throne, marking the beginning of the Tudor dynasty.

Henry VI, Part 3: The play delves into the turbulent period of the Wars of the Roses, exploring themes of ambition, power, betrayal, and the consequences of political strife. The title emphasizes the pivotal role of King Henry VI, who grapples with the challenges of maintaining a fragile kingdom amidst internal dissent and external conflicts. The play offers a glimpse into the brutality and complexity of political maneuvering during a transformative period in England's history.

RICHARD III
(1592–1593)

Act 1 - Ambitions Unveiled:

Scene 1:

Richard, consumed by insatiable ambition, embarks on a ruthless path to secure the throne by eliminating potential rivals, including his own brothers. Through cunning manipulation, he plans to wed Anne, the widow of a prince. Surprisingly, Richard succeeds in wooing her, twisting her hatred into acceptance.

Scene 2:

Anne becomes entangled in Richard's web of deceit, gradually succumbing to his persuasive tactics. Richard revels in his power to control those around him, even distorting Anne's emotions and perceptions.

Scene 3:

The ailing King Edward IV's impending demise casts a shadow over the realm, creating a tumultuous power struggle. Richard capitalizes on the chaos, orchestrating schemes to eliminate enemies and assert his dominance.

Scene 4:

Employing mercenaries, Richard engineers the execution of a nobleman held captive, falsely attributing the act to the Queen's command. In his dying moments, the nobleman exposes Richard's hand in the sinister plot.

Act 2 - Seizing Power:

Scene 1:

Clarence, imprisoned in the Tower, becomes a pawn in Richard's quest for supremacy. Manipulative as ever, Richard ensures his marriage to Anne, strengthening his claim to the throne and extinguishing potential threats.

Scene 2:

Richard's strategic manipulation of Anne leads to an unexpected conquest of her heart. His mastery of deception continues as he eliminates those who might challenge his authority.

Scene 3:

The treacherous end of Clarence marks Richard's unrelenting drive to consolidate power. With each adversary he eliminates, his grip on the throne becomes more resolute.

Scene 4:

Richard abandons his plan to marry Elizabeth of York and instead hatches a plot to wed her to strengthen his claim. Buckingham, a loyal ally, assists Richard in subverting the family of Queen Elizabeth.

Act 3 - The Reign of Tyranny:

Scene 1:

As Richard ascends the throne, his guilt and paranoia gnaw at his conscience. The consequences of his manipulations become increasingly evident, and the atmosphere of the court becomes tense and oppressive.

Scene 2:

Driven by paranoia, Richard commands the execution of perceived enemies, plunging his court deeper into a climate of fear and mistrust.

Scene 3:

Richard's machinations sow discord between him and Buckingham, who eventually turns against him. The once-faithful ally now plans a rebellion to oust the tyrant.

Scene 4:

Buckingham's rebellion crumbles under the weight of Richard's cunning. The despot's power tightens as he eliminates opponents and reinforces his dominance.

Act 4 - Battle and Desperation:

Scene 1:

Haunted by guilt, Richard's dreams torment him, revealing his inner turmoil. Meanwhile, Richmond, a rival claimant to the throne, rallies supporters for a decisive clash.

Scene 2:

Richard's efforts to maintain his dwindling support falter as his paranoia deepens. The chasm between him and his nobles widens, leaving him increasingly isolated.

Scene 3:

Richard's forces confront Richmond's army in the Battle of Bosworth, a pivotal engagement that will determine the fate of England's monarchy.

Act 5 - Downfall and Legacy:

Scene 1:

Richard fights valiantly in the Battle of Bosworth, but his downfall becomes inevitable as his forces crumble. The end of his tyrannical reign draws near.

Scene 2:

Richard meets his fate in the midst of battle, while Richmond emerges victorious. The era of Richard's brutal rule comes to an end.

Scene 3:

Richmond ascends the throne, marking a new beginning for England under the Tudor dynasty. The play concludes with a sense of hope for a brighter future.

THE COMEDY OF ERRORS (1592–1593)

Act 1 - A Tale of Twins and Tragedy:

Merchant Egeon of Syracuse journeys to Epidamn on personal business. His wife, Emilia, pregnant, stays behind. Emilia also arrives in Epidamn and gives birth to twin sons. Meanwhile, another woman gives birth to twin sons as well. Egeon buys the second set of twins from the woman to serve his own sons.

Act 2 - Twins Separated by Fate:

Egeon and his family set sail but face a storm. Egeon, with one son and a baby, and Emilia, with the other children, are separated during the chaos. Egeon's group is rescued by an Epidaurus ship, while Emilia and her sons are saved by a Corinthian ship.

Act 3 - A Comedy of Errors Begins:

Years later, Antipholus of Syracuse, raised by Egeon, travels to Ephesus with his servant, Dromio, in search of his twin brother. In Ephesus, Antipholus of Syracuse's appearance confuses everyone, leading to a series of mistaken identities.

Act 4 - Identity Confusion and Love Affairs:

Antipholus of Syracuse faces confusion as he's mistaken for his twin brother. Antipholus of Ephesus's wife begins to question his sanity, while he falls in love with her sister. Chaos ensues as identities mix up.

Act 5 - Reunion and Resolution:

The confusion escalates at a monastery where Antipholus of Ephesus takes refuge from a physician. Egeon arrives in Ephesus, recognizes his sons, and reveals their true identities. Egeon is sentenced to death due to political tensions between Ephesus and Syracuse.

As the Duke pardons Egeon and restores familial bonds, all misunderstandings are resolved. A festive gathering concludes the play, emphasizing the importance of avoiding mistakes that lead to grave consequences, and the need for effort in correcting them.

TITUS ANDRONICUS (1593–1594)

Act 1 - Triumph and Intrigue:

Scene 1: The Victorious Return

Titus Andronicus, a great warrior, returns to Rome after defeating the Goths. He brings captives, including Tamora, the Queen of the Goths, and her three sons. The Roman emperor, Saturninus, and his brother Bassianus both seek to marry Tamora.

Scene 2: Treasures of War

Titus requests that Saturninus take Tamora as his wife, allowing him to marry his daughter Lavinia to Bassianus. However, Saturninus chooses Tamora as his empress, leaving Titus shocked and disappointed.

Scene 3: The Passing of the Crown

Saturninus announces his engagement to Tamora, but she is secretly in love with Aaron, her Moorish lover. Titus supports Saturninus' claim to the throne, hoping to gain favor. Saturninus promises to marry Lavinia, but Bassianus and Lavinia elope instead.

Scene 4: Love and Deceit

Tamora plots with her sons, Chiron and Demetrius, to manipulate Saturninus and advance their power. They plan to have Demetrius marry Lavinia, thereby making her vulnerable to their schemes.

Act 2 - Betrayal and Revenge:

Scene 1: Saturninus' Choice

Saturninus confronts Titus and his family, demanding that Lavinia be returned to him. However, Titus presents his loyalty and offers his son Lucius as a token of goodwill.

Scene 2: A Sinister Alliance

Tamora, now Empress, conspires with Aaron to further her interests. She agrees to help Chiron and Demetrius marry Lavinia, thereby gaining control over her and taking revenge on Titus.

Scene 3: The Violation of Lavinia

Chiron and Demetrius brutally rape Lavinia and cut off her hands and tongue to prevent her from identifying them. Lavinia's suffering becomes a symbol of the violence and chaos engulfing Rome.

Scene 4: Blaming the Innocent

Titus is framed for the murder of Bassianus by framing two of his own sons, Quintus and Martius. They are falsely accused, arrested, and banished from Rome.

Act 3 - Unleashed Fury:

Scene 1: The Mutilation of Lavinia

Lavinia, unable to speak or write, struggles to convey her suffering to her family. She uses a stick to write the names of Chiron and Demetrius in the sand, revealing her attackers.

Scene 2: A Gruesome Message

Aaron delivers Titus a message demanding that he cut off his own hand and send it to the Emperor in exchange for his sons' lives. Titus complies and sends the hand.

Scene 3: The Vow of Vengeance

Titus, driven to madness by grief and anger, vows revenge against Tamora, Chiron, Demetrius, and Saturninus. He forms a pact with his remaining sons, Lucius and Marcus, to take down the empire.

Scene 4: The Twisted Feast

In a bizarre dinner scene, Titus serves Tamora and her family a pie containing the remains of Chiron and Demetrius. He then kills Lavinia in a sacrificial ritual to appease her spirit.

Act 4 - Schemes and Retribution:

Scene 1: The Capture of Aaron

Lucius seeks to overthrow Saturninus, while Aaron and Tamora plot to discredit Titus' claims of Tamora's crimes. Lucius captures Aaron, who reveals the truth about Tamora's children and her role in the violence.

Scene 2: The Gruesome Deaths

Aaron is ordered to bury his newborn son alive, and he reveals the location of Chiron and Demetrius' remains. Lucius captures Tamora and forces her to watch as he kills her sons.

Scene 3: A Macabre Feast

Tamora's body is stuffed into a pie and fed to Saturninus, who kills her in his rage. Titus kills Saturninus and is then killed by Lucius, who is crowned the new emperor.

Act 5 - The Final Reckoning:

Scene 1: The Fall of the Empress

Aaron is captured and sentenced to a gruesome death. Before he dies, he reveals that he fathered Tamora's child and that he has hidden the child, who represents a future threat.

Scene 2: The Death of Titus

Titus' legacy is remembered, and Lucius pardons those who helped him in his quest for revenge. The cycle of violence comes to an end with the death of Aaron and the promise of a more peaceful rule under Lucius.

Scene 3: The Final Clash

Saturninus' army faces off against Lucius' supporters in a final battle. Saturninus is killed, and Lucius emerges victorious, restoring order to Rome.

Scene 4: Lucius' Rule and Aaron's Fate

Lucius takes the throne and pledges to bring unity and stability to Rome. Aaron is buried up to his chest and left to starve to death as punishment for his crimes.

> The Legacy of Titus Andronicus: The play's brutal violence and themes of revenge serve as a cautionary tale of the consequences of unchecked hatred and the cycle of violence. It showcases the darkest aspects of human nature and the destruction that can result from vengeance. The play's sources include various ancient texts, including the works of Ovid, Euripides, and Seneca.

THE TAMING OF THE SHREW (1593–1594)

Act 1 - Sparks and Matches:

Scene 1: The Introduction

The play begins in Padua, where wealthy Baptista Minola is faced with a predicament: he can't marry off his younger daughter Bianca until her elder sister, Katherine, is wed. Suitors flock to Bianca, but Katherine's sharp tongue and fiery temperament deter potential matches.

Scene 2: Petruchio's Proposition

Lucentio, a suitor to Bianca, hatches a plan with his servant Tranio. Meanwhile, Petruchio arrives in Padua seeking a wealthy wife. Hearing of Katherine's fortune, he decides to court her, regardless of her reputation.

Act 2 - Courtship and Scheming:

Scene 1: A Tutor's Guise

Tranio, disguised as Lucentio, teaches Bianca Latin. Hortensio, another suitor to Bianca, disguises himself as a music tutor to be near her.

Scene 2: The Wooing of Katherine

Petruchio's unconventional courtship of Katherine begins. He uses reverse psychology, seeming disinterest, and humor to "tame" her fiery nature.

Act 3 - Bickering and Bonding:

Scene 1: Disguised Identities

Tranio, as Lucentio, continues to woo Bianca, while the real Lucentio assumes the role of a Latin tutor. Katherine's shrewish behavior continues, but she and Petruchio start to form a connection.

Scene 2: A Transformative Dinner

Petruchio and Katherine visit Baptista's house. Petruchio tests Katherine's patience by challenging her views on reality. He insists that the moon is the sun, and Katherine reluctantly agrees to humor him.

Act 4 - Trials and Triumphs:

Scene 1: A Comedy of Disguises

Disguises and confusion abound as Lucentio, Hortensio, and Tranio all vie for Bianca's affection. Tranio impersonates Lucentio and presents Baptista with a fake father's consent.

Scene 2: The Infamous Widow

Petruchio plans to leave for his wedding, but arrives late and in a ridiculous outfit. He insists on leaving immediately after the ceremony, skipping the feast, and enduring Katherine's anger.

Act 5 - Wedding Bells and Revelations:

Scene 1: The Bride's Test

Katherine and Petruchio head to her father's house. Petruchio tests her obedience by denying her food and new clothes until she agrees with everything he says.

Scene 2: The Betrothal of Bianca

Lucentio's true identity is revealed, and he and Bianca are betrothed. Katherine and Petruchio return, and Katherine delivers a moving speech on the duty of wives to obey their husbands.

> The Taming of the Shrew: The play explores themes of gender roles, power dynamics, and societal expectations. The title itself reflects the central conflict as Petruchio's attempts to "tame" Katherine are balanced against her transformation from a "shrew" to a submissive wife. The comedic aspects highlight the absurdity of the courtship rituals and the complexity of human relationships.

TWO GENTLEMEN OF VERONA (1594–1595)

Act 1 - Friendship and Love:

Scene 1: Verona's Streets

The play opens in Verona with the close friendship between Valentine and Proteus. Valentine is departing for Milan, while Proteus will stay in Verona due to his love for Julia.

Scene 2: Julia's Abode

Julia and Lucetta discuss Julia's affection for Proteus. Despite Lucetta's advice, Julia writes a letter to Proteus and gives it to her servant.

Act 2 - Milan's Temptations:

Scene 1: Milan - Duke's Palace

Valentine arrives in Milan, and the Duke's daughter, Silvia, falls in love with him. The Duke arranges her marriage to Thurio, though Silvia is disinterested.

Scene 2: Julia's Arrival

Julia disguises herself as a page named Sebastian and goes to Milan to find Proteus. She arrives at the moment when Proteus confesses his love for Silvia.

Scene 3: Milan - Street

Proteus reveals his newfound love for Silvia to Valentine, who encourages him to pursue her. However, Proteus is torn between his loyalty to Valentine and his growing infatuation.

Act 3 - Deception and Confusion:

Scene 1: Milan - Duke's Palace

Proteus, under the Duke's command, woos Silvia on Thurio's behalf. Silvia, mistaking Proteus for Valentine, scorns him.

Scene 2: Milan - Street

Julia, disguised as Sebastian, encounters Proteus and becomes his page. She witnesses him serenading Silvia, further deepening her heartbreak.

Act 4 - Forgiveness and Reconciliation:

Scene 1: The Outlaws' Cave

Valentine is captured by a group of outlaws, led by none other than Proteus. The outlaws plan to rob Silvia of her wealth, but Valentine pleads for her safety.

Scene 2: Milan - Duke's Palace

Julia, as Sebastian, reveals her true identity to Proteus. In a surprising twist, Proteus realizes the error of his ways and decides to reunite Valentine and Silvia.

Act 5 - Unmasking and Resolution:

Scene 1: Milan - Street

Valentine, Silvia, Proteus, and Julia come together in Milan. Proteus offers Valentine Silvia's hand, and Valentine forgives him for his betrayal.

Scene 2: Verona - Julia's House

The play concludes in Verona, where Julia and Lucetta exchange news. Proteus and Julia's love is restored, and they plan to marry.

Two Gentlemen of Verona: The play explores themes of friendship, loyalty, love, and forgiveness. It showcases the complexities of human emotions, the challenges of maintaining relationships, and the transformative power of self-awareness. The title emphasizes the bond between two friends as they navigate love and temptation in a journey that ultimately leads to reconciliation and growth.

LOVE'S LABOUR'S LOST (1594–1595)

Act 1 - Pursuit of Knowledge:

Scene 1:

King Ferdinand of Navarre and his courtiers – Berowne, Longaville, and Dumaine – pledge to dedicate three years to studying and fasting, forsaking women.

Scene 2:

Don Adriano de Armado, a Spanish nobleman, confesses his love for Jaquenetta, a country girl. Costard, a clown, delivers the letter to Jaquenetta.

Scene 3:

The King decrees that no woman should come within a mile of the court, and his courtiers reluctantly agree.

Act 2 - Letters and Entanglements:

Scene 1:

Berowne admits that the King's plan is challenging and questions its practicality. The courtiers all confess their secret affections for various women.

Scene 2:

Armado discovers Costard delivering his letter to Jaquenetta and punishes him. Berowne arrives, revealing his own letter, and they exchange letters.

Scene 3:

The Princess of France and her attendants – Rosaline,

Maria, and Katharine – arrive to discuss the surrender of Aquitaine.

Act 3 - Revelations and Affections:

Scene 1:

The Princess receives the King's letter but refuses to negotiate until the following day. The courtiers disguise themselves as Russians to visit the Princess.

Scene 2:

Armado presents a play to entertain the court. Holofernes, a pedant, and Nathaniel, a curate, assist in the performance.

Scene 3:

Berowne reveals the courtiers' true identities to the Princess and her attendants, leading to humorous interactions and newfound affections.

Act 4 - Challenges and Reflections:

Scene 1:

Berowne proposes that they break their oaths to study, and the Princess suggests a one-year waiting period before accepting the courtiers' affections.

Scene 2:

Don Adriano de Armado challenges Costard to a duel. The Princess and her attendants test the courtiers' love by swapping roles and disguises.

Act 5 - Revelations and Resolution:

Scene 1:

The courtiers serenade the Princess and her attendants, revealing their identities. Holofernes, Nathaniel, and Dull, a constable, are joined by Moth, a page.

Scene 2:

News arrives of the death of the King of France, forcing the Princess and her attendants to return immediately.

Scene 3:

The courtiers and the Princess confront each other about their feelings and the misunderstandings that have arisen.

Scene 4:

Holofernes and Nathaniel present the Nine Worthies, and Armado arrives, injured from his duel with Costard. The play concludes with festivities.

> The play "Love's Labour's Lost" explores themes of love, knowledge, and the complexities of human relationships. Set in the court of Navarre, King Ferdinand and his courtiers embark on a journey of self-discovery and romantic entanglements. The title suggests the challenges and uncertainties that come with pursuing both intellectual pursuits and matters of the heart. As the characters grapple with their own feelings and intentions, the play unfolds with witty dialogue, wordplay, and comedic situations that highlight the folly of attempting to control the unpredictable forces of love.

ROMEO AND JULIET (1594–1595)

Act 1 - Love's Beginnings and Feud:

Scene 1: Verona Streets

The play opens with a brawl between servants of the Montague and Capulet families. The Prince of Verona intervenes to halt the fight.

Scene 2: Capulet's House

Count Paris seeks Lord Capulet's permission to marry his daughter Juliet. Capulet suggests waiting for Juliet to mature. He invites Paris to a masquerade ball.

Scene 3: Montague's House

Romeo, Benvolio, and Mercutio discuss love and attend the Capulet ball in disguise. Romeo sees Juliet and instantly falls in love.

Scene 4: Capulet's Ballroom

Romeo and Juliet meet and share an instant connection. Tybalt recognizes Romeo and wants to challenge him, but Capulet stops him.

Act 2 - Hidden Love and Secrecy:

Scene 1: Verona Streets

Romeo sneaks into the Capulet orchard to see Juliet. They confess their love and make plans to marry secretly.

Scene 2: Friar Laurence's Cell

Romeo confides in Friar Laurence about Juliet. The Friar agrees to marry them, hoping their union will end the feud.

Scene 3: Verona Streets

Tybalt challenges Romeo, leading to a fight where Mercutio is killed. Romeo avenges Mercutio's death by killing Tybalt and is banished.

Act 3 - Desperate Measures and Tragic Choices:

Scene 1: Verona Streets

Romeo and Juliet spend their last night together before Romeo's banishment. They discuss their love and future plans.

Scene 2: Capulet's House

Capulet arranges Juliet's marriage to Paris, which she refuses. Nurse advises Juliet to accept the marriage.

Scene 3: Friar Laurence's Cell

Friar Laurence offers a plan to reunite Romeo and Juliet. He gives Juliet a potion to simulate death temporarily.

Scene 4: Capulet's House

Preparations for Juliet's wedding are overshadowed by her apparent death.

Act 4 - Grief and Desperation:

Scene 1: Capulet's House

The Capulets grieve Juliet's "death." Friar Laurence's plan is initiated as Juliet is placed in the family tomb.

Scene 2: Verona Streets**

Romeo learns of Juliet's "death" and rushes back to Verona, intending to die by her side.

Act 5 - Tragic Endings and Reconciliation:

Scene 1: Mantua

Friar John fails to deliver a letter to Romeo about Juliet's plan. Romeo hears of Juliet's "death" from Balthasar and hurries back to Verona.

Scene 2: Capulet's Tomb

Romeo encounters Paris at Juliet's tomb and kills him. He takes poison and dies beside Juliet.

Scene 3: Capulet's Tomb

Juliet awakens to find Romeo dead and kills herself with his dagger.

Scene 4: Verona Streets

The feud's consequences become apparent as the Montagues and Capulets reconcile.

Epilogue:
The chorus reflects on the tragic deaths of Romeo and Juliet and the hope that their story will end the feud and promote peace.

RICHARD II
(1595–1596)

Act 1 - The Dispute:

Scene 1: The King's Court

King Richard II presides over a court session where Henry Bolingbroke accuses Thomas Mowbray of treason. They are ordered to delay their duel, and Richard announces his plan to go to Ireland.

Scene 2: The Duke of Gloucester's House

Queen Isabella, Richard's uncle John of Gaunt, and Bolingbroke's father, the Duke of York, express their concerns about Richard's actions and the state of the kingdom.

Act 2 - The Exile:

Scene 1: The Duke of York's Garden

Bolingbroke laments his exile and secretly plots to return to England. The Duke of York grapples with his loyalty to Richard and sympathy for his son.

Scene 2: A Room in Ely House

News of John of Gaunt's impending death reaches Richard, who plans to seize Gaunt's lands and wealth for his own gain.

Scene 3: Gloucester's Garden

John of Gaunt delivers a powerful speech reflecting on England's decline under Richard's rule and the significance of the land's legacy.

Act 3 - The Rebellion:

Scene 1: Coventry

Bolingbroke returns to England with supporters, aiming to reclaim his inheritance. The Duke of York is torn between allegiances as he faces the growing tension.

Scene 2: The Duke of York's Palace

York attempts to mediate between Bolingbroke and Richard, but Bolingbroke's swelling forces force him to choose a side.

Scene 3: Wales

Richard arrives back in England to confront Bolingbroke's uprising. He finds his power diminished, and many nobles align with Bolingbroke.

Act 4 - The Deposition:

Scene 1: Westminster Hall

Bolingbroke is crowned King Henry IV. Richard is presented before the new king and coerced into abdicating. He reflects on his fall from grace.

Scene 2: Pomfret Castle

King Henry IV learns of Richard's demise in captivity, and his guilt over Richard's fate becomes palpable.

Act 5 - Reflection and Resolution:

Scene 1: Windsor Castle

King Henry IV grapples with internal strife and plots against his reign. He expresses remorse over his role in Richard's downfall.

Scene 2: Berkeley Castle

Henry Bolingbroke, now King Henry IV, contemplates the challenges of rule and the fragile peace he has attained.

Scene 3: Westminster Abbey

King Henry IV's reign faces threats, including the rebellion led by the Earl of Northumberland. He ponders the fleeting nature of power and its consequences.

"Richard II" chronicles the downfall of King Richard II and the ascent of Henry Bolingbroke, who becomes King Henry IV. The tensions between Richard and Bolingbroke escalate from a personal quarrel into a full-scale rebellion, ultimately leading to Richard's dethronement. The play delves into themes of authority, loyalty, and the repercussions of misrule. Richard's introspection and Henry's internal conflicts highlight the complexities of leadership and the conflicts between power and legitimacy. Through intricate language and political intrigue, Shakespeare navigates the tragic course of a monarch's rule and the transformative impact of his choices on his own destiny and the destiny of the kingdom.

A MIDSUMMER NIGHT'S DREAM (1595–1596)

Act 1 - The Enchanted Forest:

Scene 1: Athens

Duke Theseus - The noble ruler of Athens, excitedly anticipates his wedding to Hippolyta, the Queen of the Amazons. They discuss the upcoming celebrations and their own romantic history.

Hippolyta - The Queen of the Amazons and bride-to-be of Theseus. She talks with him about the swift passage of time as they eagerly await their wedding day.

Hermia - A young woman in love with Lysander. Hermia's father insists she marry Demetrius, but Hermia and Lysander plan to elope.

Lysander - Hermia's love interest. He and Hermia plan to escape Athens and marry secretly due to her father's objections.

Demetrius - A suitor to Hermia. Demetrius is loved by Helena, but he pursues Hermia despite her feelings for Lysander.

Helena - A friend of Hermia and in love with Demetrius. She feels unloved and unappreciated and is willing to reveal Hermia's plans to win Demetrius's favor.

Scene 2: A Room in Quince's House

Peter Quince - The director and organizer of a play to be performed at Theseus's wedding. He assigns roles to the amateur actors.

Act 2 - The Magical Realm:

Scene 1: The Enchanted Forest

Fairy King Oberon - Oberon and his queen, Titania, have a disagreement over the custody of a young changeling boy. Oberon decides to use a magical love potion on her.

Fairy Queen Titania - Titania refuses to give up the young changeling boy to Oberon, which causes tension between them.

Puck (Robin Goodfellow) - Oberon's mischievous servant. He is tasked with fetching a magical flower that can be used to create the love potion.

Nick Bottom - A weaver who is part of the group of actors preparing the play. Puck transforms Bottom into a comical figure with the head of a donkey.

Titania's Fairy Attendants - Servants to Queen Titania, they are tasked with attending to her and participating in the magical world.

Scene 2: The Same Place

Puck - Puck's mischief with the love potion creates confusion among the young lovers, causing them to fall in and out of love with the wrong people.

Lovers - Hermia, Lysander, Demetrius, and Helena wander into the forest and become embroiled in Puck's magical pranks.

Scene 3: The Same Place

Oberon - Oberon observes the chaos and instructs Puck to fix the lovers' romantic entanglements.

Bottom - Transformed into a donkey, Bottom becomes the object of Titania's affections when she falls under the spell of the love potion.

Act 3 - The Lovers' Trials:

Scene 1: The Same Place

Lovers - Hermia, Lysander, Demetrius, and Helena navigate the confusion caused by the love potion, leading to arguments and revelations.

Scene 2: Quince's House

Actors - The amateur actors rehearse their play, "Pyramus and Thisbe," with humorous misunderstandings and awkward performances.

Act 4 - The Play Within a Play:

Scene 1: The Enchanted Forest

Lovers - The lovers watch the amateur actors perform the play "Pyramus and Thisbe," which is filled with comedic mistakes and exaggerations.

Act 5 - The Unveiling of Magic:

Scene 1: Athens

Theseus - Theseus reflects on the play and offers a lighthearted critique, finding amusement in the actors' performance.

Hippolyta - Hippolyta shares her thoughts on the play and the nature of imagination and dreams.

> In "A Midsummer Night's Dream," Shakespeare masterfully weaves together the human and magical realms. Through the interplay of lovers' misadventures and the comical conflicts of the fairy world, the play explores themes of love, illusion, and the transformative power of imagination. The enchanting forest setting becomes a realm of whimsy and charm, where love's complexities are magnified by magic and mischief.

KING JOHN
(1596–1597)

Act 1 - The Struggle for Power:

Scene 1: King John's Court

In the grand court of King John, a tense atmosphere prevails as the monarch discusses the volatile issue of the French throne succession. Advisors counsel him on the situation, with Queen Eleanor offering her seasoned advice. The conflicting claims to the French crown set the stage for the political tensions to come.

Scene 2: The French Court

Across the Channel, King Philip of France and his mother discuss the English threat. They are steadfast in rejecting King John's claim, as King Philip fears losing his territory to the English king. This scene provides insight into the rival monarchs' motivations and sets up the impending conflict.

Act 2 - Diplomacy and Conflict:

Scene 1: King John's Court

Amid the opulence of King John's court, negotiations take place to secure peace. The proposed solution involves marrying John's niece Blanche to the French Dauphin. The stakes are high as the marriage is intended to be a bridge between England and France. This scene illustrates the importance of diplomacy in avoiding war.

Scene 2: The French Court

In the French court, King Philip discusses the marriage alliance with his mother and advisors. This is a pivotal moment as King Philip contemplates the potential for peace or continued hostility with England. The internal dynamics of the French court come to light as they weigh their options.

Act 3 - Betrayals and Alliances:

Scene 1: France

The Bastard, Philip Faulconbridge, discovers his true lineage through a letter from his deceased father. This revelation sets him on a journey of self-discovery and a quest to establish his legitimacy. His character becomes a symbol of the complexities of identity and the quest for recognition.

Scene 2: England

The tension escalates as Arthur's claim to the throne becomes a focal point. King John's willingness to execute his own nephew for the sake of maintaining power exposes the harsh realities of political ambition. Constance's grief and anger provide an emotional anchor in this scene.

Act 4 - Tragedy and Consequences:

Scene 1: England

As King John grapples with the aftermath of Arthur's death, his own internal conflict deepens. The decision to eliminate a rival claimant to the throne has lasting consequences. The scene highlights the moral dilemmas faced by leaders when their ambitions clash with their humanity.

Scene 2: France

King Philip learns of Arthur's death and realizes the gravity of the situation. The ramifications of the events in England reverberate across the Channel. King Philip's reflections underscore the interconnectedness of the European powers and the tragic toll of their power struggles.

Act 5 - Resolution and Reflection:

Scene 1: England

Tensions reach their peak as a rebellion led by Louis challenges King John's rule. The battlefield becomes a microcosm of the larger conflict, highlighting the high stakes and personal sacrifices of war. King John's struggles reflect the broader themes of the play.

Scene 2: England

The Bastard's leadership on the battlefield brings about a victory for England. His actions showcase the intersection of personal valor and broader political objectives. This scene reinforces the complexities of honor, loyalty, and duty in times of conflict.

Epilogue - The Legacy of Conflict:

Scene 1: England

As King John lies ill from poisoning, he reflects on the consequences of his decisions. His death marks the culmination of his struggles for power and the end of his era. The legacy he leaves behind is one of turmoil, revealing the destructive potential of unchecked ambition.

"King John" masterfully navigates the intricate web of power, loyalty, and ambition. Shakespeare's characters grapple with the enduring tension between personal desires and the greater good, resulting in a timeless exploration of the human condition in the context of political power dynamics.

THE MERCHANT OF VENICE (1596–1597)

Act 1 - Setting the Stage:

Scene 1: Venice - A Street

Antonio, a wealthy merchant, is melancholic without an apparent reason. His friend Bassanio seeks financial help from Antonio to woo the heiress Portia. Antonio agrees but is cash-strapped due to his ships being at sea.

Scene 2: Belmont - Portia's Estate

Portia discusses the terms of her father's will with her suitors. Her father devised a test involving caskets (gold, silver, lead), and the suitor who chooses correctly wins her hand. Portia's displeasure with this arrangement is evident.

Act 2 - Pursuits of Love and Fortune:

Scene 1: Belmont - Portia's Estate

More suitors arrive, but none successfully choose the right casket. Bassanio arrives and chooses the correct casket, winning Portia's love. Gratiano, Bassanio's friend, decides to marry Portia's lady-in-waiting, Nerissa.

Scene 2: Venice - A Street

Shylock, a Jewish moneylender, is approached by Bassanio to lend him money on Antonio's behalf. Shylock harbors resentment against Antonio and agrees, demanding a pound of Antonio's flesh as collateral.

Act 3 - The Trial and Consequences:

Scene 1: Venice - Courtroom

Shylock pursues the forfeiture of Antonio's pound of flesh in court. Portia, disguised as a lawyer, intervenes and uses legal maneuvering to save Antonio. Shylock's plot is foiled, and he faces severe consequences.

Scene 2: Belmont - Portia's Estate

Portia and Nerissa return to Belmont, and the women pretend that they were elsewhere. They reveal the rings they took from Bassanio and Gratiano, causing tension between the couples.

Act 4 - Reckonings and Reconciliation:

Scene 1: Venice - Courtroom

Antonio's ships return safely, rendering Shylock's bond void. However, Shylock's financial ruin is compounded when he is forced to convert to Christianity. Antonio's mercy spares Shylock's life, but Shylock remains devastated.

Scene 2: Belmont - Portia's Estate

Portia, still disguised as a lawyer, helps resolve the marital conflicts caused by the ring exchange. The couples reconcile, and it is revealed that Bassanio and Gratiano were tricked by their wives.

Act 5 - The Power of Mercy:

Scene 1: Belmont - Portia's Estate

News arrives that Antonio's ships are safe. Portia and Nerissa reveal their disguises and their roles in the courtroom drama. The couples rejoice in their happiness, while Lorenzo and Jessica share their own moments of love.

"The Merchant of Venice" intricately weaves themes of love, justice, and prejudice. Through its complex characters and intricate plots, the play delves into the depths of human motivations, showcasing both the light and dark aspects of humanity. Shakespeare's exploration of mercy, compassion, and the pursuit of happiness serves as a poignant reminder of the complexities of the human experience.

HENRY IV, PART 1 (1597–1598)

Act 1 - Rumblings of Rebellion:

Scene 1: King Henry's Court

King Henry IV expresses concern about his son, Prince Hal's, wayward behavior and his companionship with the boisterous Falstaff. News of a rebellion led by the Earl of Northumberland reaches the court.

Scene 2: London - The Boar's Head Tavern

Falstaff and his comrades, including Prince Hal, engage in revelry. Falstaff's humorous and cynical outlook contrasts with Hal's sense of duty and his intent to redeem his reputation.

Scene 3: Warkworth - Northumberland's Castle

The Earl of Northumberland and his son, Hotspur, plan their rebellion against King Henry IV. They discuss their grievances and alliances, setting the stage for the conflict to come.

Act 2 - Shifting Alliances:

Scene 1: London - King Henry's Court

King Henry IV receives news of the rebellion and prepares to face it. He demands Hotspur's ransom for the release of Edmund Mortimer, but his request is denied.

Scene 2: London - The Boar's Head Tavern

Prince Hal and Falstaff engage in playful banter, showcasing their complex relationship. Hal reveals his intentions to redeem his reputation and prove his worth.

Scene 3: Warkworth - Northumberland's Castle

Hotspur and his allies solidify their plans for rebellion, further fueled by their grievances against the king's administration.

Act 3 - The Clash of Forces:

Scene 1: Shrewsbury - King Henry's Camp

King Henry IV and his forces prepare to confront the rebels led by Hotspur. Falstaff, given a position of authority, reveals his lack of military discipline and his humorous outlook.

Scene 2: Shrewsbury - Rebel Camp

Hotspur and his allies rally their forces, inspired by Hotspur's fiery speeches. Hotspur's father, Northumberland, learns of his son's success in recruiting additional support.

Scene 3: Shrewsbury - Battlefield

The Battle of Shrewsbury ensues, with fierce combat between the royal forces and the rebels. Prince Hal, against his father's wishes, distinguishes himself in battle.

Act 4 - Consequences and Reflections:

Scene 1: York - Archbishop's Palace

Prince Hal reflects on the battle and the casualties. News arrives that Hotspur has been slain, raising Hal's stature in his father's eyes.

Scene 2: London - King Henry's Court

King Henry IV, while mourning the loss of Hotspur, receives news of further rebellion in Wales. He remains concerned about Hal's transformation.

Scene 3: Gaultree Forest

Falstaff, falsely claiming victory over Hotspur, accumulates credit and wealth. The darker aspects of his character are revealed through his lies and manipulations.

Act 5 - Resolution and Preparation:

Scene 1: Gloucestershire - Shallow's Orchard

Justice Shallow and Falstaff engage in humorous reminiscences. Prince Hal, now reconciled with his father, prepares to take on more serious responsibilities.

Scene 2: Westminster - King Henry's Court

King Henry IV settles affairs related to the recent rebellions and discusses his health. Prince Hal pledges to go on a pilgrimage to Jerusalem once the kingdom is stable.

"Henry IV, Part 1" presents a complex tapestry of characters and themes, exploring the nature of leadership, honor, and the challenges of reconciling personal desires with responsibilities. Through witty dialogues, intense battles, and nuanced character development, Shakespeare delves into the complexities of power and the journey towards maturity and kingship for Prince Hal.

HENRY IV, PART 2 (1597–1598)

Act 1 - A Kingdom in Transition:

Scene 1: London - King Henry's Court

King Henry IV reflects on his tenuous hold on the throne and his concerns about the kingdom's future. News arrives of rebellion in the North.

Scene 2: London - The Boar's Head Tavern

Falstaff and his companions engage in humorous banter. Falstaff's wit and disregard for morality contrast with Prince Hal's growing sense of responsibility.

Scene 3: Gloucestershire - Shallow's Orchard

Justice Shallow and Falstaff reminisce about their youth. Falstaff's exploits and exaggerations add comedic elements to the scene.

Act 2 - Continuing Struggles:

Scene 1: London - King Henry's Court

King Henry IV's health deteriorates, leading to concerns about the stability of the kingdom. Prince Hal's intentions to reform are tested by Falstaff's antics.

Scene 2: London - The Boar's Head Tavern

Prince Hal and Falstaff engage in witty exchanges, highlighting their complex relationship. Falstaff's dubious tales continue to entertain.

Scene 3: Warkworth - Northumberland's Castle

Rebellion stirs as Northumberland and other allies plan to challenge King Henry IV's rule. Rumors of the king's illness fuel their ambitions.

Act 3 - Shifting Loyalties:

Scene 1: Gloucestershire - Shallow's Orchard

Falstaff's humorous tales continue as he prepares to recruit soldiers for the king's army. The levity contrasts with the kingdom's political tensions.

Scene 2: London - King Henry's Court

King Henry IV's condition worsens, and he frets about the division among his supporters. Prince Hal promises to reform after his father's death.

Scene 3: London - The Boar's Head Tavern

Falstaff's companions share stories and jests. The tavern serves as a backdrop for the play's comedic moments and discussions on honor.

Act 4 - Resolving Conflicts:

Scene 1: London - King Henry's Court

Rumors of rebellion continue as the king's supporters discuss the kingdom's state. Prince John attempts to negotiate peace with the rebels.

Scene 2: Gloucestershire - Shallow's Orchard

Falstaff's lightheartedness contrasts with the grim reality of war. The characters reveal their anxieties about the uncertain future.

Scene 3: Coventry

The rebels gather to confront Prince John's forces. The tension between political aspirations and personal loyalties escalates in the midst of battle.

Act 5 - A New Era:

Scene 1: London - King Henry's Deathbed

King Henry IV passes away, and Prince Hal prepares to ascend the throne as King Henry V. The weight of leadership and the need for reform weigh heavily on him.

Scene 2: London - King Henry's Coronation

King Henry V vows to reform the kingdom and redeem his youthful reputation. The play ends with a sense of transition and the promise of a new era.

> "Henry IV, Part 2" continues the exploration of political intrigue, personal growth, and the challenges of leadership seen in its predecessor. The play delves into the tensions between humor and seriousness, as Falstaff's antics contrast with the kingdom's political struggles. Prince Hal's transformation into King Henry V is further developed, as he grapples with his father's legacy and the responsibilities of ruling.

MUCH ADO ABOUT NOTHING (1598–1599)

Act 1 - Whims of Love:

Scene 1: Messina - A Court

The quick-witted Beatrice engages in a spirited verbal duel with Benedick, showcasing their clever repartee and hidden affections. Their playful banter sets the tone for their evolving relationship.

Scene 2: Messina - A Court

A messenger arrives with news of the impending arrival of soldiers, including Claudio and Don Pedro. Claudio quickly becomes enamored with Hero, Leonato's daughter, while Don Pedro decides to help Claudio win her heart.

Scene 3: Messina - Leonato's House

Claudio confesses his newfound love for Hero to Benedick, who responds with his usual sharp wit. The stage is set for romantic entanglements and misunderstandings to unfold as preparations for the soldiers' arrival continue.

Act 2 - Deceptions Unveiled:

Scene 1: Messina - A Court

Don John, the illegitimate brother of Don Pedro, plots with his henchmen to deceive Claudio and disrupt the blossoming romance between him and Hero. Their manipulation threatens to undermine trust and create conflict.

Scene 2: Messina - Leonato's Garden

Benedick eavesdrops on a conversation where his friends discuss Beatrice's unspoken love for him. This revelation challenges his preconceptions and sparks introspection.

Scene 3: Messina - A Room in Leonato's House

Don Pedro and Claudio are deceived into believing that Hero is unfaithful to Claudio. Their misunderstanding leads to a public humiliation of Hero during their intended wedding ceremony.

Act 3 - Love Tested:

Scene 1: Messina - Leonato's Garden

Dogberry, the constable, and his assistant Verges are introduced, bringing comic relief with their bumbling antics. Claudio confronts Hero during the wedding ceremony, accusing her of infidelity in front of all.

Scene 2: Messina - A Church

The comedic investigation led by Dogberry and Verges uncovers the truth behind Don John's deceitful plot. The plot against Hero begins to unravel, but the revelation comes too late.

Scene 3: Messina - Leonato's Garden

Hero's innocence is proven, and Claudio realizes his mistake. The couple is reconciled, and Benedick and Beatrice's true feelings for each other are unveiled through a series of love letters.

Act 4 - Redemption and Reconciliation:

Scene 1: Messina - A Church

Borachio confesses his role in the deception, exposing Don John's villainy. Claudio publicly acknowledges his wrongdoings and offers to make amends for his actions against Hero.

Scene 2: Messina - A Garden

Amidst the chaos of Dogberry's comedy, Beatrice and Benedick confess their love for each other. With Claudio and Hero's relationship mended, the stage is set for joyful resolutions.

Act 5 - Joyful Resolutions:

Scene 1: Messina - Leonato's Garden

The final scenes unfold during a festive celebration. Claudio and Hero's wedding takes place, and the joyful news of their impending nuptials is followed by the heartwarming realization of Beatrice and Benedick's affection for one another.

Scene 2: Messina - Leonato's House

As the play concludes, the joyful atmosphere is tempered with a note of melancholy as the characters reflect on the lingering effects of Don John's treachery. Yet, the power of love and forgiveness ultimately prevails, leading to a harmonious resolution.

"Much Ado About Nothing" skillfully intertwines humor, romance, and human foibles. The interplay between Beatrice and Benedick showcases the complexities of attraction, while the theme of deception and its ultimate exposure highlights the importance of truth and trust. The play's climax is a delightful celebration of love, redemption, and second chances.

HENRY V (1598–1599)

Act 1 - The Call to War:

Scene 1: London - The Palace

King Henry V contemplates his claim to the throne of France and decides to wage war to assert his rights. He challenges the Dauphin's insulting gift of tennis balls, setting the stage for conflict.

Scene 2: London - The Palace

Henry gathers his advisors to discuss his plans for war. The ambassadors from France deliver a scornful message, further fueling his determination to invade.

Scene 3: London - A Tavern

Falstaff, a former companion of Prince Hal, has passed away. The scene shifts from politics to humor as Henry prepares to lead his troops into battle.

Act 2 - Preparing for Battle:

Scene 1: Southampton - A Street

The scene transitions to the docks of Southampton as Henry's army prepares to depart for France. He disguises himself to gauge his soldiers' opinions and rally their spirits.

Scene 2: France - Before Harfleur

Henry's forces lay siege to Harfleur. His motivational speech before the walls of the city inspires his troops to fight valiantly.

Scene 3: France - A French Camp

The French nobles discuss the impending battle and their overconfidence in their victory. Henry visits his soldiers incognito once again, sharing their hopes and fears.

Act 3 - The Battle of Agincourt:

Scene 1: France - The English Camp

On the eve of the Battle of Agincourt, Henry reflects on the weight of leadership and the responsibilities of a king. The soldiers share stories and bond before the battle.

Scene 2: France - The English and French Camps

Henry receives a disguised French nobleman and learns of the French opinion of him. As the battle draws near, the soldiers pray and Henry delivers a rousing speech.

Scene 3: France - The English and French Camps

The Battle of Agincourt commences, and the English, despite being outnumbered, achieve a surprising victory. The scene portrays the chaos, bravery, and carnage of battle.

Act 4 - Diplomacy and Romance:

Scene 1: France - Troyes

The French court contemplates peace with England. Negotiations involve marriage proposals and alliances, leading to Henry's offer to marry Princess Katherine.

Scene 2: France - A Room in the Palace

Henry's courtship of Katherine is amusingly fraught with language barriers and awkwardness. The scene highlights the human side of the king as he navigates diplomacy and love.

Act 5 - Return and Reflection:

Scene 1: England - Southampton

The play concludes with Henry's triumphant return to England. He reunites with his subjects and contemplates the burdens of kingship and the impermanence of power.

> "Henry V" portrays the transformative journey of King Henry V from a charismatic prince to a resolute monarch. The play captures the complexities of leadership, diplomacy, and warfare, presenting Henry as a charismatic yet multifaceted ruler. The rousing speeches, memorable battles, and moments of reflection showcase the challenges and triumphs of leadership, while the blend of humor and gravitas adds depth to the characters and themes.

JULIUS CAESAR (1599–1600)

Act 1 - The Conspiracy Begins:

Scene 1: Rome - A Street

The commoners celebrate Caesar's triumph, while the tribunes criticize his popularity. Flavius and Marullus remove decorations from Caesar's statues, highlighting the tension between the masses and the authorities.

Scene 2: Rome - The Forum

Caesar announces his intention to participate in the Lupercal festival and dismisses Calpurnia's ominous dreams. Cassius expresses his concerns about Caesar's growing power to Brutus.

Scene 3: Rome - A Street

Cinna the poet is mistakenly attacked by a mob who believe he is Cinna the conspirator. This foreshadows the chaos and confusion that will unfold in Rome.

Act 2 - The Plot Unfolds:

Scene 1: Rome - Brutus's Garden

Brutus contemplates the idea of killing Caesar for the greater good. Cassius manipulates him into believing that Caesar's ambition threatens the republic.

Scene 2: Rome - Caesar's Palace

Calpurnia pleads with Caesar not to attend the Senate meeting due to her unsettling dreams. Decius convinces Caesar to go, playing on his ego and ambition.

Scene 3: Rome - A Street

Artemidorus tries to warn Caesar of the conspirators' plan through a letter, but Caesar dismisses his concerns.

Scene 4: Rome - Brutus's House

The conspirators gather and finalize their plan to assassinate Caesar. Brutus argues that they must kill him for the sake of Rome's future.

Act 3 - The Assassination:

Scene 1: Rome - The Capitol

On the Ides of March, the conspirators surround Caesar and assassinate him. Brutus justifies their actions to the crowd, while Mark Antony seizes the opportunity to turn public opinion against them.

Scene 2: Rome - The Forum

Mark Antony delivers a stirring funeral speech that turns the crowd against the conspirators. The people riot, seeking revenge on those responsible for Caesar's death.

Act 4 - Civil Strife:

Scene 1: Rome - A House

The conflict between the conspirators and Mark Antony escalates into civil war. Brutus and Cassius argue over strategy and personal differences, foreshadowing their eventual downfall.

Scene 2: Rome - A Camp near Alexandria

Brutus and Cassius continue to clash over their leadership roles and the state of their armies. Their personal animosities begin to weaken their alliance.

Act 5 - The Tragic End:

Scene 1: Philippi - The Plains of Philippi

The armies of Brutus and Cassius face off against those of Octavius and Antony. Both sides prepare for battle, and the tension is palpable.

Scene 2: Philippi - The Field of Battle

Brutus and Cassius are defeated in the Battle of Philippi. Cassius dies by suicide, believing he has been betrayed. Learning of Cassius's death, Titinius also takes his own life.

Scene 3: Philippi - Another Part of the Field

Brutus's forces are overwhelmed, and he decides to end his own life rather than be captured. Strato assists Brutus in his suicide, and Octavius and Antony reflect on the outcome.

> "Julius Caesar" delves into the complex dynamics of ambition, loyalty, and political manipulation. The play examines the consequences of unchecked power, showcasing how the assassination of a leader can lead to chaos and civil strife. The characters' internal struggles, their moral dilemmas, and their ultimate fates demonstrate the fragility of human relationships and the destructive

nature of political ambitions. Through its exploration of history and human psychology, "Julius Caesar" remains a timeless exploration of the complexities of leadership and the price of political change.

AS YOU LIKE IT (1599–1600)

Act 1 - The Court and the Forest:

Scene 1: The Court

Duke Frederick banishes his niece Rosalind from the court. Celia, Rosalind's cousin, decides to join her in exile. Orlando challenges the wrestler Charles and gains the attention of Rosalind.

Scene 2: The Forest of Arden

Rosalind and Celia disguise themselves and venture into the forest. Rosalind adopts the name Ganymede, while Celia becomes Aliena. They encounter Orlando, who hangs verses dedicated to Rosalind on trees.

Act 2 - Love and Deception:

Scene 1: The Forest

Duke Senior, in exile, reflects on the beauty of nature. Jaques, a melancholic nobleman, philosophizes on life. Orlando leaves verses on trees expressing his love for Rosalind.

Scene 2: The Forest

Rosalind (disguised as Ganymede) meets Orlando and offers to cure him of his love by pretending to be Rosalind. Silvius pines for Phoebe, who falls in love with Ganymede.

Act 3 - Romance and Reconciliation:

Scene 1: The Forest

Touchstone, a jester, marries Audrey. Rosalind (Ganymede) teaches Orlando about true love. Oliver reveals his transformation from a villain to a changed man in love.

Scene 2: The Forest

Jaques meets Duke Senior's group and engages in a philosophical discussion about the nature of life. Orlando rescues Oliver from a lioness, and Oliver becomes reconciled with him.

Scene 3: The Forest

Phoebe continues to pursue Ganymede, unaware of Ganymede's true identity. Rosalind, as Ganymede, devises a plan to resolve the romantic tangles.

Act 4 - Love's Confusions:

Scene 1: The Forest

Orlando, unaware of Rosalind's true identity, courts her as Ganymede. Silvius continues to pine for Phoebe, who remains infatuated with Ganymede.

Scene 2: The Forest

Touchstone and Audrey meet Corin and discuss the complexities of love and marriage. Rosalind arranges a mock wedding to expose the absurdity of love and courtship.

Act 5 - Reunion and Revelations:

Scene 1: The Forest

Phoebe, Silvius, Orlando, and Rosalind (as Ganymede) meet. Rosalind reveals her true identity to Orlando, and Phoebe realizes her love for Silvius.

Scene 2: The Forest

Hymen, the god of marriage, arrives to preside over the multiple weddings. Rosalind and Orlando, Celia and Oliver, Silvius and Phoebe, and Touchstone and Audrey all get married.

> "As You Like It" delves into issues of love, identity, and nature's transformational power. The play, set against the backdrop of Arden's forest, presents a whimsical analysis of the intricacies of love relationships as well as the contrast between courtly life and the simplicity of ature. The characters' self-discovery journeys, humorous wordplay, and examination of various aspects of love make "As You Like It" a joyful and thought-provoking comedy. The play's blend of romance, comedy, and philosophical speculations continues to captivate audiences, prompting them to reflect on the nature of love and the human experience.

TWELFTH NIGHT (1599–1600)

Act 1 - Shipwrecks and Deceptions:

Scene 1: A Coast in Illyria

A shipwreck separates Viola from her twin brother Sebastian. Believing him to be dead, Viola disguises herself as a man named Cesario and enters the service of Duke Orsino.

Scene 2: The Court of Duke Orsino

Orsino sends Cesario (Viola) to woo Olivia on his behalf. Olivia, mourning her brother's death, rejects Orsino's advances but becomes infatuated with Cesario.

Scene 3: Olivia's House

Sir Toby Belch and his companions, including Maria and Sir Andrew Aguecheek, revel and cause mischief. Maria writes a letter to Malvolio, Olivia's steward, as part of a prank.

Act 2 - Disguises and Misunderstandings:

Scene 1: The Sea Coast

Viola and Sebastian are both alive but unaware of each other's survival. Viola, as Cesario, continues to woo Olivia for Orsino, while Sebastian encounters Antonio, a sea captain who saved him.

Scene 2: Olivia's House

Malvolio receives the prank letter, which leads him to behave strangely and believe that Olivia loves him. Olivia and Cesario (Viola) have a conversation, during which Olivia's affection for Cesario deepens.

Scene 3: The Street

Sir Andrew and Cesario (Viola) duel, but Antonio intervenes, mistaking Cesario for Sebastian. Antonio is arrested, and Viola realizes her brother is alive.

Act 3 - Love's Confusions:

Scene 1: Olivia's Garden

Olivia openly declares her love for Cesario (Viola), but Cesario reveals her true identity and tries to dissuade Olivia's feelings. Malvolio appears in cross-gartered yellow stockings, believing they are Olivia's preference.

Scene 2: A Room in Olivia's House

Sir Toby, Maria, and Feste continue to mock Malvolio, who is locked in a dark room and declared mad. Cesario (Viola) returns to Orsino and begins to realize her own feelings for him.

Scene 3: Sebastian and Antonio

Sebastian and Antonio arrive in Illyria. Sebastian, thinking his sister drowned, agrees to accompany Antonio to Duke Orsino's court.

Act 4 - Mistaken Identities and Reunions:

Scene 1: Olivia's Garden

Olivia, mistaking Sebastian for Cesario (Viola), asks him to marry her. Sebastian, confused but willing, agrees.

Scene 2: The Street

Mistaking Sebastian for Cesario (Viola), Sir Andrew and Sir Toby challenge him to a duel. Sebastian easily defeats them, and Antonio is arrested when he intervenes.

Act 5 - Revelations and Resolutions:

Scene 1: Olivia's House

Viola reveals her true identity to Orsino, and Olivia explains her marriage to Sebastian. The twins are reunited, and the confusion over their identities is cleared up.

Scene 2: Orsino's Palace

Sebastian and Olivia arrive at Orsino's palace, and Viola and Sebastian are finally reunited. Orsino realizes his love for Viola, and the play concludes with multiple marriages.

> "Twelfth Night" is a delightful comedy of mistaken identities, disguises, and romantic entanglements. Set in the whimsical world of Illyria, the play explores themes of love,

self-discovery, and the transformative power of appearance and reality. The intricate web of misunderstandings and the play's colorful characters, including the witty Viola, the lovesick Orsino, and the mischievous Feste, create a joyful and humorous atmosphere. With its themes of gender identity and the complexity of love, "Twelfth Night" continues to captivate audiences, offering both laughter and reflection on the intricacies of human relationships.

HAMLET (1600– 1601)

The place of action is Elsinore Castle

Act 1 - The Ghost's Revelation:

Scene 1: The guard platform

Guards encounter a ghost resembling the late King Hamlet at Elsinore Castle. They tell Horatio, a friend of Hamlet, about it. Horatio is skeptical, and they decide to inform Hamlet, who decides to see the ghost himself.

King Hamlet's death has left the throne to his brother Claudius, who has married Hamlet's widow, Queen Gertrude. Prince Hamlet is deeply affected by his mother's quick remarriage, expressing his grief and disillusionment.

Scene 2: The same place

The guards tell Hamlet and Horatio about the ghost, and they witness the ghost's appearance. Hamlet decides to speak to the ghost alone, learning that it is his father's spirit, revealing that he was murdered by Claudius.

Scene 3: The state room

Hamlet reveals to his friends that he has learned the truth about his father's death. He swears them to secrecy and determines to feign madness as he plans his revenge.

Act 2 - Spying and Deceit:

Scene 1: Polonius' room

Polonius advises his daughter Ophelia to avoid Hamlet's

advances and dismisses Hamlet's affections as insincere.

Scene 2: Reception hall.

Claudius sends Rosencrantz and Guildenstern, Hamlet's childhood friends, to spy on him. Hamlet quickly deduces their motives and feigns madness.

Scene 3: The same place

Hamlet suspects Polonius and Claudius are using Ophelia to spy on him. He delivers his famous soliloquy, "To be or not to be," contemplating life and death.

Scene 4: At the gates of Elsinore

Hamlet encounters actors who have arrived at the castle. He asks them to perform a play reenacting King Hamlet's suspected murder, aiming to gauge Claudius's reaction and confirm his guilt.

Act 3 - Unmasking Deceit:

Scene 1: Reception hall

Hamlet's play, "The Mousetrap," confirms Claudius's guilt. Claudius's reaction validates Hamlet's suspicions.

Scene 2: Gertrude's chamber

Hamlet confronts his mother in her chamber, angrily accusing her of betrayal and indirectly killing Polonius, who was hiding behind the curtains.

Scene 3: Reception hall

Claudius, concerned for his safety, plans to send Hamlet to England with Rosencrantz and Guildenstern. Hamlet discovers their intention and switches the sealed letter for his own.

Scene 4: The same place

Ophelia's grief over Polonius's death has caused her to go mad. She exhibits erratic behavior and sings disjointed songs, prompting concern from those around her.

Act 4 - Tragedy Deepens:

Scene 1: Reception hall

Claudius learns of Hamlet's return to Denmark and his killing of Polonius. He conspires with Laertes to manipulate a fencing match to kill Hamlet.

Scene 2: The courtyard of Elsinore Castle

Hamlet's ship to England is intercepted by pirates, and he returns to Denmark, unaware of the plot against him.This becomes known from the letter that the servant gives to Horatio.

Scene 3: Reception hall

Laertes and Claudius conspire to kill Hamlet during the fencing match using a poisoned rapier and a poisoned cup.

Scene 4: In the vicinity of Elsinore Castle

Hamlet encounters Fortinbras's army en route to attack Poland. He reflects on the purpose of war and his own procrastination, recognizing the need for action.

Scene 5: From the conversation between Gertrude and Claudius, it is revealed that Ophelia is dead; she drowned.

Act 5 - Fatal Showdown:

Scene 1: The churchyard of Elsinore Castl

Hamlet, Horatio, and Queen Gertrude witness Ophelia's funeral. Hamlet and Laertes confront each other, leading to a scuffle at her grave.

Scene 2: Reception hall

The fencing match between Hamlet and Laertes takes place. Laertes's poisoned rapier strikes Hamlet, and in the ensuing chaos, Gertrude and Laertes die.

Scene 3: The same place
Hamlet fatally wounds Claudius with the poisoned rapier, avenging his father's death. Hamlet himself succumbs to the poison and dies.

Scene 4: The same place
Hamlet's dying request to Horatio is to share his story. Fortinbras arrives to take control of the throne, ending the play with a sense of resolution and change in power.

"Hamlet" by William Shakespeare delves into various profound philosophical themes. It contemplates existentialism through Hamlet's iconic soliloquy, questioning the value and significance of life. Death and mortality are central as the play explores the nature of death, the afterlife, and the fear of the unknown. The dichotomy between reality and appearance is examined as characters like Claudius and Polonius present facades that differ from their true selves. The interplay of free will and fate is evident as Hamlet wrestles with the concept of agency versus predestination. The blurred line between madness and sanity is highlighted through Hamlet's feigned madness and Ophelia's genuine descent into insanity. Ethical inquiries arise as revenge clashes with justice, prompting contemplation on the morality of vengeance. The theme of corruption parallels the decay of the Danish court and prompts reflections on societal moral decline. Moral dilemmas, duty, responsibility, and introspection into identity contribute to the play's profound exploration of human nature and the complexities of existence.

THE MERRY WIVES OF WINDSOR (1600–1601)

Act 1: Mischief in Windsor

Scene 1: A street in Windsor

Sir John Falstaff, a roguish knight, hatches a plan to woo two wealthy married women, Mistress Page and Mistress Ford, in hopes of financial gain. He sends them identical love letters.

Act 2: Love's Complexities

Scene 1: A room in the Garter Inn

The two wives discover Falstaff's duplicity and conspire to teach him a lesson. Meanwhile, their husbands suspect Falstaff's advances and plan to thwart him.

Act 3: Pranks and Promises

Scene 1: A street in Windsor

Falstaff's comical attempts to woo the wives continue, leading to amusing misunderstandings and hidden identities.

Scene 2: A room in Page's house

Anne Page, daughter of the Pages, faces pressure from her parents to marry the suitor they have chosen for her, but she is in love with Fenton.

Act 4: Falstaff's Follies

Scene 1: The same place

Falstaff is duped into disguising himself as the "Black Witch of Brentford" by the wives' prank. He ends up being ridiculed and thrown into a ditch.

Scene 2: The same place

More comedic confusion ensues as Falstaff gets involved in a laundry basket escape plan.

Act 5: Joyful Resolutions

Scene 1: A street in Windsor

The town gathers for a masked ball, leading to further confusion and misunderstandings among the characters.

Scene 2: Before Page's house

Everything comes to a head at Herne's Oak, where all deceptions are revealed, and Falstaff is publicly humiliated.

Scene 3: The same place

Anne Page marries Fenton against her parents' wishes, but they ultimately give their blessing. Falstaff is left to reflect on his folly and the mirthful chaos that unfolded.

In "The Merry Wives of Windsor" Shakespeare presents a lighthearted comedy filled with mistaken identities, witty pranks, and the triumph of love and laughter over deception. The characters' interactions and the amusing situations they find themselves in showcase Shakespeare's skill in creating a delightful and entertaining play.

TROILUS AND CRESSIDA (1601–1602)

Act 1: Setting the Stage

Scene 1: The Trojan camp during the ongoing Trojan War

The Trojan War rages on, and the Greek leaders debate their strategy. Troilus, a Trojan prince, is in love with Cressida, the daughter of a Trojan priest.

Act 2: Love and Betrayal

Scene 1: The Trojan camp

Troilus and Cressida's blossoming romance is hindered by the war's chaos. Cressida is traded to the Greeks in exchange for a Trojan prisoner, causing heartache.

Scene 2: Inside the walls of Troy

Pandarus, Cressida's uncle, plays matchmaker between her and Troilus. Meanwhile, the Greek leaders continue to plot their course of action.

Act 3: War and Politics

Scene 1: The Greek camp

The Greek and Trojan leaders debate a possible truce, but it ends in failure due to mistrust and pride.

Scene 2: Various locations

Troilus and Cressida's love is tested as they navigate the challenges of the war and its political intrigues.

Act 4: Deception and Discord

Scene 1: Outside the Trojan walls

Troilus witnesses Cressida's apparent betrayal when she is seen with the Greek warrior Diomedes.

Scene 2: Inside the Greek camp

Achilles' pride and reluctance to fight become apparent as he quarrels with the Greek leaders, and the war's brutality is further exposed.

Act 5: Tragedy and Reflection

Scene 1: The battlefield

The war intensifies, and Troilus seeks revenge on Diomedes. Tragedy strikes as Hector, a Trojan hero, is killed by Achilles.

Scene 2: Inside the Trojan walls

Troilus' love for Cressida turns bitter as he confronts her about her supposed infidelity. The play concludes with a sense of disillusionment and the haunting question of the value of honor and love in times of war.

> "Troilus and Cressida" delves into the complexities of love, honor, and politics amidst the backdrop of the Trojan War. Shakespeare's exploration of human nature, moral ambiguity, and the consequences of war is intertwined with the tragic and often disillusioning experiences of the characters.

The play challenges conventional notions of heroism and portrays the harsh realities of a world torn by conflict.

ALL'S WELL THAT ENDS WELL (1602–1603)

Act 1: A Difficult Proposition

Scene 1: Helena's house

Helena, the intelligent and compassionate daughter of a skilled physician, confesses her profound love for Bertram, a nobleman. Despite the societal divide between them, she approaches the King of France to seek his assistance in winning Bertram's affection.

Act 2: Healing and Deception

Scene 1: The French court

Helena embarks on a journey to the French court with the intention of curing the ailing King. Armed with her father's medical knowledge, she offers her skills to heal the monarch. In gratitude, she seizes the opportunity to ask for Bertram's hand in marriage.

Scene 2: Possibly a room where Bertram is located or a location outside the palace

Bertram, while agreeing to wed Helena, harbors doubts and plots an escape. He devises intricate and nearly unattainable conditions for their marriage, secretly hoping to evade the commitment.

Act 3: Pursuit and Transformation

Scene 1: Various locations on Helena's journey

Determined to win Bertram's heart, Helena pursues him to distant lands, determined to fulfill his stringent conditions. Her unwavering determination drives her to confront various obstacles along the way.

Scene 2: A room in the palace

Parolles, Bertram's charismatic yet flawed friend, faces a pivotal moment of exposure. His true colors are revealed as he is unmasked as a braggart and a coward. The characters' genuine natures begin to surface, offering glimpses into their complexities.

Act 4: Deceptions Unraveled

Scene 1: A room in the palace

Helena ingeniously unravels Bertram's deception, laying bare his betrayal and manipulation. Seeking the King's justice, she unveils the truth and seeks a resolution to their situation.

Scene 2: Possibly a location within the camp

Parolles experiences a humiliating downfall as he is exposed by his comrades and left to fend for himself. Bertram, confronted with his own shortcomings, confronts the consequences of his actions and takes the first steps toward self-improvement.

Act 5: Resolution and Reconciliation

Scene 1: The court of the palace

Bertram, transformed by his experiences, returns to France. Helena's relentless pursuit and unwavering virtue lead to a touching reconciliation between the two. Their marriage becomes a symbol of overcoming trials and adversities.

Scene 2: The same place

The play concludes with the titular phrase, "All's well that ends well." This sentiment encapsulates the notion that despite the challenges faced, a positive resolution has been achieved. The characters' growth and newfound understanding pave the way for a brighter future. Shakespeare's exploration of love, perseverance, and personal development resonates through the triumphant conclusion.

MEASURE FOR MEASURE (1604–1605)

Act 1: A Request for Justice

Scene 1: A room in the Duke's palace

The Duke of Vienna entrusts his authority to Angelo, his deputy, and secretly disguises himself as a friar to observe the city's affairs. Angelo enforces strict moral laws, which leads to the arrest of Claudio for impregnating his lover Juliet out of wedlock.

Act 2: A Proposal and a Plan

Scene 1: A room in a convent

Isabella, Claudio's virtuous sister, pleads for her brother's life. She appeals to Angelo's sense of justice, but he offers her a morally questionable proposition: Claudio's freedom in exchange for her virginity.

Scene 2: Another room in the Duke's palace

The Duke, disguised as a friar, intervenes and guides Isabella to consider accepting Angelo's offer to save her brother. He begins to orchestrate a complex plan to bring about justice and expose the truth.

Act 3: Deceit and Discovery

Scene 1: A street

Claudio's friend Lucio tries to convince Isabella to change her mind, but she remains resolute in her decision to preserve her chastity. The Duke, as the friar, continues to manipulate events behind the scenes.

Scene 2: Another room in the Duke's palace

Angelo, consumed by his desires and guilt, propositions Mariana, his former betrothed, for a secret liaison. The Duke uses Mariana to execute his plan for exposing Angelo's hypocrisy.

Act 4: Trials and Temptations

Scene 1: The prison

The Duke, as the friar, convinces Isabella to trick Angelo by agreeing to his proposal but sending Mariana in her place. Meanwhile, Claudio faces execution, and his life hangs in the balance.

Scene 2: Another room in the prison

Angelo's moral dilemma intensifies as he believes he is consummating his union with Isabella but is, in reality, with Mariana. The discovery of this ruse sets the stage for a climactic confrontation.

Act 5: Reckoning and Redemption

Scene 1: A room in the Duke's palace

The Duke unveils his true identity, and the characters confront the consequences of their actions. Angelo is exposed for his hypocrisy, and Isabella's virtue remains intact.

Scene 2: The same place

The Duke's verdicts bring resolution to the tangled web of deceit and manipulation. He offers forgiveness and mercy to some while punishing others, ultimately demonstrating the complex interplay between justice and compassion.

Scene 3: The same place

The play ends with the Duke proposing marriage to Isabella, a surprising twist that prompts reflection on the nature of authority, morality, and human relationships. "Measure for Measure" delves into the depths of morality and power, challenging societal norms and exploring the complexities of human behavior.

OTHELLO (1604–1605)

Act 1: Venice in Love

Scene 1: A street in Venice

Roderigo expresses his unrequited love for Desdemona to Iago, who harbors resentment toward Othello for promoting Cassio over him. Iago hatches a scheme for revenge.

Scene 2: The council chamber in Venice

The Duke of Venice and senators discuss the Turkish threat. Othello, a Moorish general, reports on his successful defense of Cyprus. Desdemona defends her love for Othello to her father, Brabantio.

Act 2: Deceit Takes Root

Scene 1: A street in Venice

The Turks are defeated, and Othello's marriage to Desdemona is celebrated. Iago's malicious plans continue as he sows seeds of doubt in Othello's mind about Desdemona's loyalty.

Scene 2: Another street in Venice

Iago convinces Cassio to ask Desdemona to intervene on his behalf to regain his position. Iago exploits this interaction to further manipulate Othello's suspicions.

Act 3: Jealousy Unleashed

Scene 1: A room in the castle

Iago plants seeds of jealousy in Othello's mind by making him believe that Desdemona is unfaithful with Cassio. Othello becomes consumed by doubt and anger.

Scene 2: Another room in the castle

Othello's jealousy intensifies, and he questions Desdemona about her involvement with Cassio. Desdemona tries to ease his fears, unaware of Iago's sinister plan.

Act 4: Manipulation and Tragedy

Scene 1: The bedchamber in the castl

Iago continues to manipulate Othello by presenting a handkerchief that belonged to Desdemona, planted in Cassio's possession. This seemingly trivial object becomes a catalyst for catastrophe.

Scene 2: Another room in the castle

Othello's jealousy spirals out of control. Iago convinces him that Desdemona is unfaithful, and Othello decides to kill her. Meanwhile, Roderigo becomes a pawn in Iago's plans.

Act 5: Tragic Resolution

Scene 1: A bedroom in the castle

Othello confronts Desdemona, who pleads her innocence. Othello smothers her to death. Emilia, Desdemona's maid and Iago's wife, uncovers the truth about the handkerchief.

Scene 2: Another room in the castle

Othello learns the full extent of Iago's deceit and realizes the tragic consequences of his actions. He kills himself. Emilia exposes Iago's villainy before being murdered by him.

Scene 3: Yet another room in the castle

Iago's treachery is revealed, and he is apprehended. Othello's tragic downfall prompts reflection on themes of jealousy, manipulation, and the destructive power of unfounded suspicion.

"Othello" remains a harrowing exploration of human emotions and the devastating impact of jealousy. But it is also worth noting Othello's incredible gullibility towards Iago. This leitmotif was often noted in the works of Konstantin Stanislavsky, who himself performed the role of Othello in his theater.

KING LEAR
(1605–1606)

Act 1: A Divided Kingdom

Scene 1: A room in the King's palace

King Lear announces his plan to divide his kingdom among his daughters based on their professions of love. Goneril and Regan offer extravagant flattery, while Cordelia speaks honestly but is disinherited. The loyal Kent is banished for opposing Lear's decision.

Scene 2: The Earl of Gloucester's castle

The Earl of Gloucester learns about Lear's actions and supports his legitimate son, Edgar. Edmund, his illegitimate son, schemes to exploit the situation and usurp Edgar's position.

Act 2: Betrayal and Suffering

Scene 1: Goneril's palace

Kent, now in disguise, offers his service to Lear, who seeks refuge with Goneril. Lear confronts Goneril's disrespectful treatment and begins to unravel emotionally.

Scene 2: Another room in Goneril's palace

Gloucester informs Edmund about a plot to protect King Lear. Edgar disguises himself as "Poor Tom," a mad beggar, to evade his father's anger and deception.

Act 3: Descent into Madness

Scene 1:A heath

Lear's mental state continues to deteriorate, and he curses Goneril. Kent's true loyalty becomes evident when he intervenes on Lear's behalf.

Scene 2: Another part of the heath

Gloucester falls victim to Edmund's betrayal and is blinded as punishment. Edgar, still disguised as "Poor Tom," helps his father through his suffering.

Act 4: Tragedy Deepens

Scene 1: A hovel in the heath

Lear and Cordelia are imprisoned by Goneril and Regan. Cordelia's unwavering love for her father shines through, and Lear begins to comprehend the depth of his errors.

Scene 2: Another part of the heath

Edgar, still in disguise, rescues his father from the depths of despair. Gloucester's suffering prompts a transformation towards redemption and self-awareness.

Act 5: Cataclysmic Conclusion

Scene 1: A room in the Duke of Albany's palace

The rivalry between Goneril and Regan reaches its peak, resulting in their deaths. Edmund's deceit is exposed, and he is fatally wounded in a duel.

Scene 2: Another room in the Duke of Albany's palace

Lear and Cordelia are captured, and despite a rescue

attempt, Cordelia is tragically hanged. Lear's grief becomes overwhelming, and he dies holding his beloved daughter.

Scene 3: Another room in the Duke of Albany's palace

Albany takes charge in the aftermath and vows to restore order to the kingdom. Kent reveals his true identity before passing away. Edgar emerges as a hero and a symbol of hope for the future.

> "King Lear" delves into profound themes of power dynamics, family relationships, mental decline, and the tragic consequences of unchecked pride. The play's heartbreaking narrative underscores the fragile nature of human bonds and the destructive outcomes of betrayal and ambition.

MACBETH (1605–1606)

Act 1: Ambition and Supernatural Forces

Scene 1: A desolate place

Three witches gather in a desolate place and prophesy Macbeth's rise to power. Their predictions set in motion a chain of events that will lead to tragedy.

Scene 2: A camp near Forres

Macbeth and Banquo, two brave Scottish generals, receive news of their victories in battle. They encounter the witches, who make prophecies that spark Macbeth's ambition.

Act 2: Murder and Guilt

Scene 1: A court within Macbeth's castle

Macbeth debates whether to commit regicide to fulfill the witches' prophecy. His wife, Lady Macbeth, encourages him to murder King Duncan and seize the throne.

Scene 2: The same place

After committing the murder, Macbeth is haunted by guilt and hallucinations. Lady Macbeth works to cover up their actions, and suspicion grows.

Act 3: Unraveling Ambitions

Scene 1: A park near the palace

Macbeth becomes increasingly paranoid and orders the murder of Banquo and his son Fleance. However, Fleance escapes, leaving a potential threat to Macbeth's rule.

Scene 2: A room in the palace

At a banquet, Macbeth is tormented by the ghost of Banquo. Lady Macbeth tries to maintain appearances but is troubled by her husband's behavior.

Act 4: Rising Tensions

Scene 1: A dark cave

Macbeth seeks further prophecies from the witches and learns of his potential downfall. He resolves to eliminate all threats, including Macduff's family.

Scene 2: A room in Macduff's castle

Lady Macduff and her children are brutally murdered by Macbeth's henchmen, reinforcing the play's themes of violence and betrayal.

Act 5: Tragic Conclusion

Scene 1: A room in the castle

Lady Macbeth's guilt and madness consume her, leading to her tragic death. Macbeth's hold on power grows more precarious as opposing forces gather.

Scene 2: The country near Birnam Wood

Macbeth faces Macduff in a final battle, where the witches' prophecies unravel. Macduff reveals that he was born by Caesarean section, foiling Macbeth's belief that he is invincible.

Scene 3: Another part of the field

Macbeth's death at the hands of Macduff solidifies the play's themes of ambition, power, and the consequences of unchecked desires.

> "Macbeth" masterfully explores the destructive effects of ambition, guilt, and the corrupting influence of power. The interplay between the supernatural, psychological turmoil, and political intrigue creates a haunting narrative that delves into the darker aspects of human nature.

ANTONY AND CLEOPATRA (1606–1607)

Act 1: Passion and Power

Scene 1: Alexandria. A room in Cleopatra's palace

Mark Antony, a Roman general, is captivated by Cleopatra, the Queen of Egypt. Their passionate love affair sets the stage for a tale of romance and political turmoil.

Scene 2: Rome. A room in Antony's house

Antony receives news of his wife's death and is urged to return to Rome. However, he is torn between his responsibilities in Rome and his infatuation with Cleopatra.

Act 2: Political Intrigue

Scene 1: Messina. A room in Pompey's house

Back in Rome, Octavius Caesar, Antony's fellow triumvir, clashes with Antony over political matters. Antony's devotion to Cleopatra creates tensions within the Roman leadership.

Scene 2: Alexandria. A room in Cleopatra's palace

Antony and Cleopatra's love deepens as they continue to navigate the complexities of their relationship. Their actions have far-reaching consequences on both personal and political levels.

Act 3: Conflict and Betrayal

Scene 1: A room in Cleopatra's palace

Octavius and Antony's rivalry escalates, leading to a naval battle at Actium. Cleopatra's actions during the battle raise suspicions of her loyalty to Antony.

Scene 2: Another room in Cleopatra's palace

Antony's forces are defeated, and he blames Cleopatra for his losses. Cleopatra, fearing Antony's anger, takes refuge in her tomb, leading Antony to believe she has died.

Act 4: Tragedy Unfolds

Scene 1: A room in Cleopatra's palace

Antony, distraught over Cleopatra's apparent death, takes his own life. Learning of this, Cleopatra is devastated and decides to join him in death.

Scene 2: Cleopatra'spalace

Cleopatra's suicide is carried out by an asp, a venomous snake. Octavius discovers her lifeless body and reflects on the fall of both Antony and Cleopatra.

Act 5: Finality and Legacy

Scene 1: A room in Cleopatra's palace

Octavius plans Cleopatra's extravagant funeral and contemplates the end of an era. He expresses his desire to parade Cleopatra's defeat through the streets of Rome.

Scene 2: Another room in Cleopatra's palace

Cleopatra's loyal handmaidens, Charmian and Iras, die by suicide to avoid capture by Octavius. Cleopatra's death marks the end of an era and the beginning of a new chapter in Roman history.

"Antony and Cleopatra" weaves together themes of love, power, politics, and the clash of cultures. Shakespeare's portrayal of the passionate yet tragic relationship between Antony and Cleopatra explores the complexities of loyalty, ambition, and the enduring allure of both love and power.

CORIOLANUS (1607–1608)

All the action takes place in Rome.

Act 1: The Great Warrior

Scene 1: A street near the gate

Caius Martius, a valiant Roman soldier, leads his troops in a battle against the Volsces. His military prowess earns him respect but also stirs resentment among the citizens of Rome.

Scene 2: A public place

Martius is honored with the name "Coriolanus" for his victory at Corioles. He returns to Rome, where political tensions and class conflicts are on the rise.

Act 2: Political Maneuvering

Scene 1: The Forum

Coriolanus is urged to enter politics and stand for consul. However, his pride and disdain for the common people make him an unpopular choice.

Scene 2: Another part of the Forum

Coriolanus's political aspirations are met with opposition from the tribunes, representatives of the plebeians. He clashes with them and rejects their demands.

Act 3: Betrayal and Exile

Scene 1: A street

Coriolanus's enemies exploit his arrogance to turn the people against him. He is banished from Rome, becoming an outcast.

Scene 2: A camp near Rome

Coriolanus seeks refuge among the Volsces, the very people he once fought against. He forges an alliance with them and prepares to lead an attack on Rome.

Act 4: A Dangerous Alliance

Scene 1: Rome. Before the gates

Coriolanus and the Volsces march towards Rome, putting the city in grave danger. His former friends plead with him to spare the city, but his anger drives him forward.

Scene 2: A camp of the Volsces

Coriolanus's mother, Volumnia, and his wife, Virgilia, visit him, begging him to end the siege. Their emotional pleas almost sway him, but his pride remains unyielding.

Act 5: Tragic Resolution

Scene 1: Rome. A public place

A peace treaty is negotiated between Rome and the Volsces, avoiding further bloodshed. Coriolanus returns to the Volsces, who become suspicious of his loyalty.

Scene 2: The Volsces' camp

Despite his earlier alliance, Coriolanus is declared a traitor by the Volsces and is assassinated. His death brings a tragic end to a life marked by military valor, political strife, and personal conflict.

"Coriolanus" delves into themes of honor, pride, political manipulation, and the tension between individualism and societal expectations. Through the character of Coriolanus, Shakespeare explores the complexities of loyalty, identity, and the destructive consequences of hubris. The play offers a powerful portrayal of a proud warrior who finds himself torn between his duty to the state and his own sense of self-worth.

TIMON OF ATHENS (1607–1608)

Act 1: A Generous Patron

Scene 1: A hall in Timon's house

Timon, a wealthy and generous nobleman of Athens, hosts a lavish banquet for his friends, showering them with gifts and kindness.

Scene 2: A servant's apartment

Timon's steward, Flavius, warns him about his excessive spending and urges him to be cautious. Timon dismisses his concerns and continues his extravagant lifestyle.

Act 2: Betrayal and Isolation

Scene 1: A Senator's house

Timon's creditors demand repayment of his debts, but he has no funds left. He turns to his friends for help, but they all refuse to assist him.

Scene 2: A banqueting room in Timon's house

Feeling betrayed and abandoned, Timon retreats to the wilderness outside Athens. He discovers a hidden cache of gold and becomes bitter and misanthropic.

Act 3: The Cynical Philosopher

Scene 1: A deserted place

Timon encounters various characters in the wilderness, including the cynical philosopher Apemantus. Timon expresses his disdain for humanity and gives away his newfound wealth.

Scene 2: Before Timon's cave in the woods

Alcibiades, an Athenian general, is banished from the city and seeks revenge. Timon offers his support to Alcibiades, further isolating himself from society.

Act 4: Reckoning and Consequences

Scene 1: The Senate House

Back in Athens, the city is plagued by political unrest and corruption. Alcibiades leads a rebellion against the city, and Timon's former friends face the consequences of their actions.

Scene 2: Before Timon's cave

Timon's creditors, realizing his newfound wealth is worthless, confront him in the wilderness. Timon rejects their pleas and continues his life of solitude and bitterness.

Act 5: Tragic Endings

Scene 1: The walls of Athens

As Alcibiades lays siege to Athens, Timon discovers the tomb of Alcibiades's lover, the prostitute Phrynia. He encounters the ghosts of his past, reflecting on his downfall.

Scene 2: A country near Athens

Timon's death is reported to the citizens of Athens. Alcibiades, now in control, reflects on Timon's fate and delivers a eulogy for the fallen nobleman.

> "Timon of Athens" is a play that explores themes of wealth, friendship, betrayal, and the corrupting influence of money. Through

the transformation of Timon from a generous patron to a bitter recluse, Shakespeare critiques the superficiality and hypocrisy of human relationships. The play portrays the consequences of unchecked greed and the harsh realities of a world driven by self-interest.

"PERICLES" (1608–1609)

Act 1: A Royal Journey Begins

Scene 1: Antioch. A room in the palace

King Antiochus reveals a sinister secret to those who seek his daughter's hand in marriage. Pericles, Prince of Tyre, solves the puzzle and discovers the truth.

Scene 2: Tyre. An ante-chamber in the palace

Pericles decides to flee Antioch and sets sail for other lands. He arrives in Tarsus and learns of the famine threatening the city.

Act 2: Love and Loss

Scene 1: Pentapolis. A room in the palace

Pericles arrives in Pentapolis and competes in a tournament for the hand of Thaisa, daughter of King Simonides. He wins her love and marries her.

Scene 2: A ship at sea.

A storm at sea threatens Pericles's ship as he sails with his pregnant wife. Thaisa seemingly dies while giving birth to a daughter, Marina, and her body is cast overboard.

Act 3: Separation and Rediscovery

Scene 1: Tarsus. An open place near the sea-shore

Pericles leaves Marina in the care of Cleon and Dionyza in Tarsus before continuing his journey. Thaisa's body washes ashore and is revived by Cerimon.

Scene 2: Ephesus. A room in Cerimon's house

Marina grows up in Tarsus, beloved by all except Dionyza. Pericles, unaware of his wife's survival, mourns her loss and continues his adventures.

Act 4: Trials and Reunion

Scene 1: Mytilene. A street before the brothel

Marina is kidnapped by pirates and sold into prostitution in Mytilene. She uses her intelligence and virtue to maintain her innocence and hope.

Scene 2: Tyre. A room in the Governor's house

Pericles arrives in Mytilene, where he encounters Marina. They are tearfully reunited, and Pericles learns of his wife's survival.

Act 5: Joyful Endings

Scene 1: Ephesus. Before Cerimon's house

Pericles reunites with Thaisa in Ephesus. The goddess Diana appears in a dream, guiding the family toward happiness.

Scene 2: Tyre. A room in the palace

Pericles and his family return to Tyre, where they are welcomed by their people. The play concludes with a sense of restoration, reconciliation, and hope.

> "Pericles" is a play filled with themes of love, separation, resilience, and redemption. The narrative takes audiences on a journey across different lands and emotional highs and lows. Through the trials and tribulations faced by Pericles and his family, the play explores the human capacity for endurance, the power of

love and virtue, and the ultimate triumph of good over adversity.

CYMBELINE (1609–1610)

Act 1: A Royal Dilemma

Scene 1: Britain. The garden of Cymbeline's palace

King Cymbeline's daughter, Imogen, secretly marries Posthumus Leonatus, prompting the king's anger. He banishes Posthumus and arranges a marriage for Imogen with Cloten.

Scene 2: Rome. Philario's house

The villainous Iachimo makes a bet that he can seduce Imogen. He travels to Posthumus with a plan to deceive him.

Act 2: Deceptions Unveiled

Scene 1: Britain. A bedchamber in Cymbeline's palace; a woman's apartment

Imogen discovers Iachimo in her bedroom, attempting to prove her fidelity to Posthumus by showing her in a compromising situation. She remains virtuous.

Scene 2: Britain. A hall in Cymbeline's palace

Posthumus, believing Imogen to be unfaithful, sends a letter to his servant Pisanio ordering him to kill her. Pisanio, however, spares her life.

Act 3: Trials and Vengeance

Scene 1: Wales. A mountainous country, with a cave

Imogen, disguised as a boy named Fidele, travels to Milford Haven, where she meets Belarius and her lost brothers Guiderius and Arviragus.

Scene 2: Before the cave of Belarius

Cloten follows Imogen to Wales, where he is killed by Guiderius in a quarrel.

Scene 3: A forest near the cave

Meanwhile, Posthumus meets a Roman army and decides to join them to fight against Britain.

Act 4: Reckonings and Reunions

Scene 1: Another place in the forest near the cave

Imogen, believing Posthumus to be dead, takes a sleeping potion administered by Pisanio. Posthumus is captured and imprisoned by the British forces.

Scene 2: Before the cave of Belarius

Imogen awakens beside the seemingly dead body of Cloten, which she mistakes for Posthumus. She encounters Lucius, the Roman leader, and joins his cause.

Act 5: Resolutions and Revelations

Scene 1: Britain. The Roman camp

Cymbeline's forces face defeat in battle, and he agrees to make peace with the Romans. Imogen and Posthumus are reunited.

Scene 2: Britain. A field of battle between the British and Roman camps

The truth about the characters' identities and actions

is revealed. Iachimo confesses to his deception, and the family members are reconciled.

Scene 3: Britain. A room in Cymbeline's palace

Cymbeline discovers his long-lost sons and their true lineage. The play ends with a joyful reunion and the promise of a brighter future.

"Cymbeline" is a complex and fantastical play that weaves together themes of love, deception, loyalty, and forgiveness. The narrative is filled with twists and turns, mistaken identities, and unexpected reunions. Throughout the play, characters face trials and challenges that test their faith in one another and their ability to overcome adversity. The resolution of the conflicts brings about a sense of unity and restoration, showcasing the power of love and the potential for redemption.

THE WINTER'S TALE
(1610–1611)

Act 1: Jealousy and Accusations

Scene 1: Sicilia, a kingdom ruled by King Leontes

King Leontes of Sicilia becomes consumed by jealousy, suspecting that his wife, Queen Hermione, is having an affair with his childhood friend King Polixenes of Bohemia.

Scene 2: Sicilia, within the palace

Leontes' suspicion intensifies, and he orders his loyal servant Camillo to poison Polixenes. Instead, Camillo warns Polixenes and they both flee to Bohemia.

Act 2: The Perils of Perdita

Scene 1: Sicilia, a court of justice within the palace

Leontes accuses Hermione of infidelity and orders her trial. Despite Hermione's protests, she is declared guilty and imprisoned.

Scene 2: Sicilia, a room in the prison

Hermione gives birth to a daughter, Perdita, in prison. Leontes refuses to acknowledge her as his child and orders Antigonus to abandon her in a distant land.

Act 3: New Beginnings in Bohemia

Scene 1: Bohemia, a place near the Shepherd's cottage

Perdita, now a young woman, lives in Bohemia as a shepherdess. She falls in love with Florizel, the son of Polixenes, who disguises himself as a commoner to court her.

Scene 2: Bohemia, before the Shepherd's cottage

Polixenes discovers Florizel's intentions and opposes their relationship. The couple decides to flee to Sicilia, seeking Leontes' approval.

Act 4: Reunions and Revelations

Scene 1: Sicilia, a room in the palace

In Sicilia, Leontes still mourns for his lost wife and daughter. Paulina, Hermione's loyal friend, reveals a statue that resembles Hermione.

Scene 2: Sicilia, another room in the palace

Perdita, Florizel, and Polixenes arrive in Sicilia. Leontes learns of their identity and reconciles with Polixenes. The statue of Hermione comes to life, and the truth is revealed.

Act 5: Healing and Redemption

Scene 1: Sicilia, another room in the palace

The joyful reunions continue as Perdita is revealed to be Leontes' daughter. Leontes begs Hermione's forgiveness for his past actions.

Scene 2: Sicilia, another room in the palace

As the play concludes, Leontes and Polixenes celebrate their newfound friendship. Perdita and Florizel are engaged, and the kingdom is united in harmony and renewal.

"The Winter's Tale" is a play that explores themes of jealousy, redemption, and the power of time to heal wounds. The story begins with a tragic misunderstanding driven by Leontes' irrational jealousy, which leads to a series of heart-wrenching events. However, as the play progresses, the power of love, forgiveness, and the passage of time brings about healing and reconciliation. The transformation of Leontes from a jealous and tyrannical ruler to a remorseful and redeemed father serves as a central arc in the narrative. The play's title itself underscores the cyclical nature of life, suggesting that even in the coldest of times, the warmth of human emotions can ultimately triumph over adversity.

THE TEMPEST (1611–1612)

Act 1: Shipwreck and Stranded

Scene 1: A ship at sea

A violent storm causes a ship carrying nobles, including Alonso, the King of Naples, to crash on a deserted island. The shipwrecked passengers fear for their lives.

Scene 2: An island

On the island, Prospero, the rightful Duke of Milan, reveals that he orchestrated the storm and saved the passengers. He tells his daughter Miranda about their past and plans for revenge.

Act 2: Plots and Magic

Scene 1: Another part of the island

Caliban, a deformed creature and servant of Prospero, curses his master. Meanwhile, Alonso's son Ferdinand is separated from the group and encounters Miranda, leading to a blossoming romance.

Scene 2: Another part of the island

Ariel, a spirit under Prospero's control, uses magic to torment Alonso's group, causing confusion and fear.

Act 3: Manipulations and Revelations

Scene 1: Another part of the island

Prospero tests Ferdinand's sincerity and subjects him to harsh labor. Ariel manipulates Alonso's group further, leading them to believe their sins are catching up to them.

Scene 2: Another part of the island

Caliban, Alonso's jester Trinculo, and the drunken butler Stephano plan to overthrow Prospero, but their plans are thwarted by Ariel's illusions.

Act 4: Forgiveness and Reunion

Scene 1: Another part of the island

Prospero confronts Alonso's group and reveals his identity. He forgives them for their past wrongdoings and arranges for Ferdinand and Miranda's marriage.

Scene 2: Another part of the island

Prospero stages a magical masque for Ferdinand and Miranda, celebrating their union. Meanwhile, Ariel reports that Caliban, Trinculo, and Stephano have been punished.

Act 5: Freedom and Farewell

Scene 1: Another part of the island

Prospero confronts his enemies and confronts the limits of his power. He forgives them and breaks his staff, renouncing magic. Ariel is set free.

Scene 2: Another part of the island

The stranded group leaves the island on a ship summoned by Ariel. Prospero delivers a final soliloquy, asking the audience to release him from the enchantment.

"The Tempest" is a play that delves into themes

of power, manipulation, forgiveness, and the transformative power of art. The narrative unfolds on a mystical island where Prospero, a wronged Duke, wields his magical abilities to orchestrate events and seek retribution against those who betrayed him. Throughout the play, Prospero's manipulation of the shipwrecked nobles raises questions about the ethical use of power and the pursuit of vengeance. c Ariel's magical interventions underscore the tension between freedom and servitude, while Caliban's complex relationship with Prospero highlights issues of colonization and oppression. Ultimately, "The Tempest" concludes with a resolution that emphasizes the power of forgiveness, the liberation from power struggles, and the potential for renewal and reconciliation.

HENRY VIII
(1612–1613)

Act 1: Political Intrigues and Marriage Proposals

Scene 1: London. A room in the Duke of Buckingham's palace

The Duke of Buckingham expresses concern about Cardinal Wolsey's growing influence. The King announces a lavish banquet where the French ambassador will propose a marriage alliance between England and France.

Scene 2: A room in the palace

Cardinal Wolsey manipulates the King to gain more power. Queen Katherine and the King's advisor, Lord Chamberlain, discuss the King's intentions for the banquet.

Act 2: The King's Dilemma

Scene 1: An ante-chamber in the palace

The King is captivated by Anne Bullen (Boleyn) and becomes infatuated with her. Wolsey sees this as an opportunity to advance his own interests.

Scene 2: An apartment of the Queen's

Queen Katherine's trial begins, where she defends her marriage to the King. Wolsey and Buckingham plot against Anne, aiming to discredit her.

Act 3: Fall of Buckingham

Scene 1: A hall of justice

Buckingham is arrested on false charges of treason. He reflects on his past and laments his downfall before his execution.

Scene 2: An ante-chamber in the palace

The King starts to doubt Wolsey's intentions and realizes his growing attachment to Anne. The King's secretary, Cromwell, becomes more prominent in court affairs.

Act 4: The King's Marriage and Wolsey's Downfall

Scene 1: A street leading to the palace

The King marries Anne secretly, and Cranmer, the Archbishop of Canterbury, blesses their union. Wolsey's influence wanes, and he falls out of favor.

Scene 2: Kimbolton. Queen Katherine's apartment

Wolsey's schemes unravel as his political opponents expose his corruption. The King realizes the truth and banishes Wolsey from court.

Act 5: Birth and Hope

Scene 1: London. A room in the palace

Queen Anne gives birth to Princess Elizabeth. The King and Anne are overjoyed, seeing this as a sign of God's favor.

Scene 2: Westminster. A street

Cranmer foresees a bright future for Princess Elizabeth and England under her rule. The play ends on a note of hope and anticipation.

"Henry VIII" delves into the intrigues, power

struggles, and personal lives of the Tudor court during King Henry VIII's reign. The play explores the political machinations of Cardinal Wolsey, who aims to consolidate his influence through manipulation and alliances. The central focus of the play is on the King's tumultuous relationships and marriages, particularly his infatuation with Anne Boleyn, which ultimately leads to his separation from Queen Katherine and the establishment of the Church of England. The downfall of Buckingham and Wolsey showcases the volatility of courtly favor and the consequences of political ambition. Additionally, the play addresses themes of divine providence and hope for a prosperous future through the birth of Princess Elizabeth. While not as frequently performed as some of Shakespeare's other works, "Henry VIII" provides a glimpse into the dramatic events and characters that shaped English history during this period.

TWO NOBLE KINSMEN (1612–1613)

The play is set in Athens

Act 1: Friendship and Love

Scene 1: Before a temple

Palamon and Arcite, cousins and best friends, are captured and imprisoned during a battle. They both fall in love with Emilia, a beautiful princess, from their prison cell.

Scene 2: A room in the palace

Emilia's decision to become a nun complicates Palamon and Arcite's feelings for her. They agree to maintain their friendship despite their shared love.

Act 2: Love's Conflicts

Scene 1: A garden outside the jail

Emilia struggles with her feelings as both Palamon and Arcite declare their love for her. A jailer's daughter falls in love with Palamon and becomes obsessed.

Scene 2: Another part of the jail

The jailer's daughter's infatuation with Palamon grows stronger, and she becomes increasingly unstable. Arcite is released from prison but is banished from Athens.

Act 3: A Tournament of Love

Scene 1: A room in the jail

Arcite disguises himself and returns to Athens to win Emilia's love. A tournament is announced, and both Palamon and Arcite compete for Emilia's hand.

Scene 2: A field of battle between the Athenian and Theban camps

The tournament begins, and both Palamon and Arcite fight valiantly. Arcite wins, but he is mortally wounded. He dies expressing his love for Emilia.

Act 4: Love's Resolution

Scene 1: A room in the jail

Palamon wins Emilia's heart after Arcite's death. The jailer's daughter's mental state deteriorates, and she creates a makeshift shrine for Palamon.

Scene 2: The country near Athens

The jailer's daughter's madness escalates, and she tries to drown herself. The Duke of Athens intervenes, and her sanity is restored.

Act 5: Resolution and Reconciliation

Scene 1:

The Duke pardons the jailer's daughter, and Palamon and Emilia's wedding is planned. Emilia and the jailer's daughter visit a temple to pray.

Scene 2:

The jailer's daughter prays for her own happiness and for the well-being of Palamon and Emilia. The play ends with a sense of closure and reconciliation.

"Two Noble Kinsmen" explores themes of friendship, love, and loyalty. The play centers around the relationship between Palamon and Arcite, two noble kinsmen who are imprisoned together and later become rivals for the love of Emilia. Their internal conflict between their friendship and their love drives much of the drama in the play. The character of the jailer's daughter provides a secondary storyline, delving into the effects of unrequited love and obsession. The play also features elements of Greek mythology and chivalric romance, with the tournament serving as a central event that tests the characters' valor and resolves the love triangle. "Two Noble Kinsmen," a collaboration between Shakespeare and John Fletcher, offers a unique blend of tragic and comedic elements, making it an intriguing addition to the Shakespearean canon.

Dear Readers,

Thank you for joining us on this journey through Shakespeare's timeless world. We hope you found our summaries insightful and engaging, whether they introduced you to Shakespeare's works or helped refresh your memory. If you enjoyed our book and found it helpful, we kindly ask for your support in the form of positive reviews on Amazon. Your *feedback not only encourages us but also assists us in continuing to create content that resonates with readers like you.*

With gratitude,
Caleb J. Sullivan

Printed in Great Britain
by Amazon

33584358R00086